THE
PICNIC
COOKBOOK

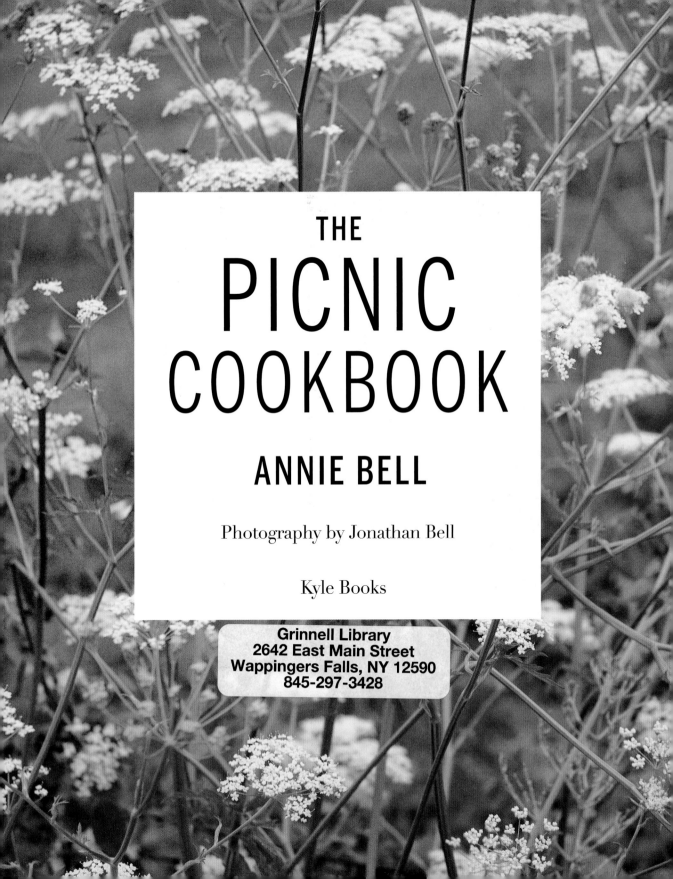

THE
PICNIC
COOKBOOK

ANNIE BELL

Photography by Jonathan Bell

Kyle Books

Published in 2013 by Kyle Books

First published in Great Britain in 2012 by
an imprint of Kyle Cathie Limited
www.kylebooks.com

Distributed by National Book Network
4501 Forbes Blvd., Suite 200
Lanham, MD 20706
Phone: (800) 462-6420
custserv@nbnbooks.com

ISBN: 978-1-906868-91-8

Library of Congress Control Number: 2013930409

Editor: Vicky Orchard
Design: Jenny Semple
Photography: Jonathan Bell
Food and Props Styling: Annie Bell
Production: Gemma John and Nic Jones

Color reproduction by ALTA London
Printed and bound by Toppan Leefung Printing Ltd in China

ACKNOWLEDGMENTS Another summer of fun spent out of doors, made possible by the many people who
helped to make *The Picnic Cookbook* happen. With many thanks firstly to my agent Lizzy Kremer at David
Higham, my sounding block, for her advice and for being there. To Kyle for all her support and giving us
the opportunity. To Vicky Orchard, Editor, for calmly steering the idea from conception to publication. Nikki
Sims for copy-editing the book. Jenny Semple for the clarity of her design. Salima Hirani for proof-reading
the manuscript. Vanessa Bird for her index. Julia Barder, as Sales and Marketing Director. Victoria Scales,
for publicity. Lastly to my favorite companion on any picnic, my husband Jonnie, for his enthusiasm and his
charming pictures and snaps. And to our long-suffering son Louis, his friends, and our friends and
relations, who gamely got into the picnic spirit and joined us on many locations.

CONTENTS

GREAT LOCATION, GREAT FOOD

"Where shall we meet for lunch?"

are six small words that send me into a tizzy. Finding good food is one thing, finding a great location another. Never one to embrace the mundane, my ideal is most likely either to be on the seventh floor of a building with panoramic views of the capital and revolve, or it's in the center of a garden of Eden gently lit by lights concealed in the flowering bougainvilleas surrounding our table, where we can dine to the backing vocals of cicadas.

In my dreams. Which is why I adore going on picnics. Before we get to the food (and fear not you have 170 pages following this musing on nothing else), picnics are about place. It is the magic seasoning and surprise and the unpredictability that leads to having fun that makes them potentially some of the most memorable dining experiences. It is only once you have dreamed up the setting and designed the stage that you can actually start to plan what you are going to eat. If I think back over the picnics I have been on, they are mapped out in my memory as a series of postcards of where we have eaten. The windswept beach with its white sand and piercing blue sky where we sheltered from the elements between boulders encrusted with barnacles and draped with seaweed. Or the springtime meadow of wild flowers when the tallest person in the party played St. Christopher by carrying the fainthearted across the shallow mountain stream that stood in the way. But there are city postcards too—the bench of a zoo in Bangkok and the shade of an orange tree in Seville; it's a great way of exploring the delis, grocery stores, and street markets of any place you happen to be visiting in the world.

Yet so often I find myself reading about picnics that go wrong. How can a picnic go wrong? Well I sort of know what you mean. I am thinking back to when, as impoverished students, my husband and I went to Paris for a few days. The first picnic opportunity provided itself on the deck of a ferry across the English Channel, which to our unworldly innocence could have been the port side of a cruise ship for all its glamour. Well, we sat and sunned ourselves with our gin and tonics and egg mayonnaise rolls, as our conversation was drowned out by the vibrating hum of the engine room. So far, so romantic.

Arriving in Paris, having taken in the Centre Pompidou we went in search of a boutique hotel, which we had chosen for its proximity to a lively street market selling the sort of French food that had lured us in the first place. We dropped off our luggage and shopped for a picnic that we could eat in the Tuileries Garden, and then it started raining, and raining. The obvious tack was to retreat to our hotel room, which we hadn't actually inspected at that point, but it seems George Orwell had been there before us in *Down and Out in Paris and London*: the "narrow street, a ravine of tall, leprous houses lurching towards one another in queer attitudes" and "the walls were as thin as matchwood, and to hide the cracks they had been covered with layer after layer of pink paper, which had come loose." Except that ours was nicotine brown. As I unwrapped our surprise package of cheeses, the exchange with the vendeuse in the market floated back, "Vous voulez le chevre bien fort?" "Mais oui," I had replied as our picnic took on ever more profound Orwellian dimensions and the pervading scent of rank, sharp goat cheeses filled the damp room with its low rafters. But you

What's the plan?

know what, given the distance in years, I now look back on it fondly.

When it comes to picnics I am a glass-half-full person. Admittedly I had to give goat cheese a rest for a while, but these days nicotine-stained wallpaper doesn't come into it and my mind wanders to blue skies, an ambient breeze and the shade of a tree, a blanket on which to sprawl, laughter, relaxation, and great food. In short, lunch or dinner in the location of your dreams or the dining room of your choosing.

Perhaps most of all I love picnics for their accessibility. They are a great leveler: they are open to anyone and everyone. You don't even have to do all the work yourself; the best in spirit are the sum of the parts where everyone brings something along and you all feast together. There is a delicious innocence about the whole experience, from the enthusiasm of plotting and planning where to go, what to pack, what to eat, what to do when you get there, and who to go with. It's an adventure.

While we may not be able to control the elements, even the simplest of picnics benefit from planning. Perhaps the main faux pas is to assume that it is about grab a blanket, a baguette, and a few cold meats and go. What we can do is maximize the chances of a picnic's success with a bit of forethought. Make sure that we have the requisite cooler bags if it's a hot day, and remember to freeze the ice packs the night before. And to pack the corkscrew, of course; on principle, I won't take a screw-top bottle on a picnic, which would ruin the challenge of not forgetting it.

And in addition, there are a few tips that as a veteran picnicker I feel make a difference. Taking two blankets, or more, instead of assuming that all five of you can comfortably lounge on one blanket, with lunch for company. The average picnic blanket is probably the size of a double bed, so work on the basis that one is bliss, two is cozy, but three is definitely a crowd. And why not give lunch its very own blanket or cloth, which does away with the hazard of sitting on it?

What shall we eat?

At last we come to the essential issue of what to eat. While there may be different types of picnic, they are all rustic affairs at heart that involve getting down and dirty in the literal sense, and as such the call is for relaxed and bohemian cooking. If you can't imagine eating it lying down, it probably doesn't fit. If it's a particularly special or more formal picnic, you may want to extend this to include knives and forks or even a trestle table, a cloth, and chairs, but the food itself still needs to be casual. So even though what follows attempts to cover every picnic scenario, there is only one style of food, because only one style works.

As to type of picnic, broadly speaking there are three scenarios into which most will fall. First off there are spontaneous last-minute picnics. Next up from that are communal get-togethers, and more ambitiously special-occasion fine-dining ones. Depending on which category your picnic is likely to fall into, which in turn will come with its own set of practical considerations, this will suggest the best menu. But all of what follows is designed to be simple, not least because I find it is easy to get carried away when planning picnics.

The walls of my home have been removed and therefore I can invite as many people as I choose. I am no longer worried about whether I have enough space at the table. Enough plates? No problem, we can take paper ones, and likewise glasses; and no need for cutlery because I'll plan for things that can be eaten with fingers. Suddenly what started out as a modest gathering is a party. But this is one of the great plusses—it's the spontaneity that makes them the occasions that they are.

LET'S GO

This is the seriously quick option. You can shop cleverly for lovely breads, cold cuts and cheeses, a few pickles, a bag of salad greens, and a carton of tomatoes and go. This kind of food involves the minimum of preparation, and makes for one of the easiest types of picnic. So, every chapter starts with suggestions for instant ideas, goodies to buy in, or those that require the simplest possible attention before you leave.

For instance, you can whisk up a salad dressing using a couple of ingredients, and take a bunch of watercress or bag of corn salad; buy some packaged dips, such as hummus and tzatziki, but give them a twist at home and put them in a slightly more alluring container than their plastic supermarket tub. There are lots of ideas for desserts too, marriages of ingredients that will bring out the best in each other, whether pears with Manchego, or dates with some gooey Gorgonzola.

PASS IT AROUND

On from the instant picnic in terms of ease are those finger foods that can be passed around, no cutlery called for, which is the demand of most

communal get-togethers, be it a sports day, street party, or a big birthday—occasions when everyone brings a plate or two of something. This tends to take a bit more time in the kitchen, but at least it is all said and done in advance. This could be anything from chicken thighs baked with lemon and za'atar, to Boston lettuce leaves filled with egg mayonnaise and strips of anchovy, or slices of Spanish tortilla, some cherry tomato and Parmesan tarts, finishing off with a decadent chocolate cake.

FINE DINING

Lastly, there are the more ambitious types of picnic that involve plates, knives, and forks. And there are occasions when this is the call, that opera or "fête champêtre" when it is good to have some ideas up your sleeve. A plate of gravlax with salad, a rack of lamb that can be sliced into delicate pink chops alongside a potato salad. When you do manage to pull it off, it can be completely magical, a glass of chilled Champagne in hand as the sun disappears and solar lanterns hung in the trees start to glow.

MIX AND MATCH

In reality, a lot of the time what suits will end up being a mélange of all three types of picnic. Probably my favorite opportune weekend picnic, waking up on a beautiful summer morning with nothing planned, is to roast a chicken and buy a loaf of sourdough, some peppery green leaves, and different tomatoes on the vine. Whisk your chicken wrapped in foil from oven to blanket, where still slightly warm an hour or two later you can hack it into rustic slivers using a folding knife, and dip the bread and salad greens in the juices. But just as simple, you could buy some salami and baked ham, but make a lovely tomato salad or tabbouleh to go with them. In short, there are all sorts of halfway houses where you're not going to the trouble of preparing every dish, but cooking or preparing just one offering will give the picnic heart and soul over and above if you had bought absolutely everything prepared.

Will it, Won't it Rain?

BEFORE

Typical. No sooner had I planned for a picnic this weekend and invited everyone but they announced a "break" in the fine September weather. As a consequence I have been glued to the local weather forecast for the last few days. On Wednesday they predicted "heavy rain," on Thursday they downgraded it to "light rain," and on Friday they upped it back up to "heavy rain," adding in "gusting winds." Today? "Light rain" apparently, so who knows?

But the plan is, we all meet in the park by the cedars and the statues, where we have a lovely lunch of baked ham and chicken, hummus, guacamole, slow-roast tomatoes and charbroiled broccoli, salt caramel millionaire's shortbread, polka dot cookies, blueberries, and figs, all washed down with ginger beer, pink lemonade, pomegranate juice, and hard cider, before playing a competitive round of volleyball. It is going to have to rain very hard before I cancel.

AFTER

I must have done something good in my life (a long, long time ago) because the rain never appeared. Or as a friend put it, "How much did you pay and to whom?" After all that fretting, the weather was lovely, sunny, ambient, and autumnal; pretty much perfect in fact. I didn't even forget anything. The only hitch was that when we laid our roast chicken, still hot from the oven, down on the blanket, it sparked the equivalent of the twilight barking of *101 Dalmations*, as word spread through the local canine population that dinner was served, and within minutes there were pooches flying at us from every direction. That aside, we won—the volleyball game and the food from the dogs.

PERFECT PICNIC: TOP TIPS

GET AHEAD

The majority of picnics take place at lunchtime. The light, the warmth, even sun we hope. Given that we not only have to pack up and to make our way there (and unpack), the more that can be done in advance, the better.

If it's a planned picnic (as opposed to a spontaneous last-minute one), reading through recipes as far as possible in advance to see whether there is anything that can be done the night beforehand, or even frozen, makes sense.

Try to spend a bit of time the evening before baking any goodies, making salad dressing, preparing crudités, packing the picnic basket, and so forth. And remember to chill any drinks, and to pop the ice packs in the freezer.

CHOOSING A MENU

Go through the motions of transporting the food before you decide on the menu (there must be an app for this). A plate of something to pass round might work if you are going to eat close to where you have parked, but if you have to negotiate a stile and lug it across several fields, it will feel like an egg-and-spoon race. Again if you are using public transport, this is going to be a no-no.

And then there is the time factor. A lovely roast whisked from your kitchen to the park and eaten slightly warm within a couple of hours may not meet the demands of packing up a picnic in the morning when you are driving any distance to a play or opera and will be eating early evening.

THINK SMALL AND LIGHT

Picnics inevitably involve carrying, so the lighter the better. I favor cooler bags over boxes, and baskets over hampers, and try to keep any real china to a minimum. Try not to take more than you need of any one commodity; a chutney, mustard, or other relish can be repackaged in Lilliputian-size jars, while salt and pepper can be scrunched up in an envelope of parchment paper.

STAYING COOL

Cold water: Take a thermos of ice water with plenty of ice cubes in it. On a really hot day, that sip of mountain-cold water will be nirvana.

Wine and drinks: Err on the side of caution here and chill your drinks below the temperature you want to drink them at before leaving (an hour in the freezer should do it), which will allow for the opening and closing of the cooler bag.

Ice packs: Remember to put these into the freezer the night before.

Wine chiller sleeve: If you double up on the chilling by popping the bottle of wine into a chiller sleeve and then inside a cooler bag, you should cover yourself in a heatwave.

Ice: For a very hot day, fill a drinks or food thermos with ice cubes.

KEEPING WARM

Blankets: It is the easiest thing to underestimate how cold it can be (or become) after that swim in the sea on a picnic, when you are snug at home and the sun is shining through the kitchen window. I swear by lightweight fluffy fleece blankets that double as picnic blankets, ditto old-fashioned woollen car blankets.

Hot drinks: Picnics have a habit of taking on a sudden chill late afternoon, or when a cloud passes over and the breeze picks up, and there is nothing quite as civilized or restorative as a mug of warm hot chocolate, coffee, or tea.

CHECK THE CHECKLIST

I don't need much of an excuse to make a list but have a particular fondness for checklists and swear by consulting them as I am packing up. There is always something that I will have thought of at some point and then forgotten about.

PICNIC FAUX PAS

● Glasses with stems—why waste good wine?
● Old blankets with holes and stains—we're not pets. If you wouldn't use it indoors, it won't do for outdoors. And you deserve a lovely new picnic blanket.
● Too much melamine and plastic—soulless "en masse," just some mixed in with the real china.
● Too much real china—too heavy, and fragile, but

a few to provide a bit of glamour and risk.
● Vintage thermoses—these need to work; looking pretty is optional.
● Ugly plastic containers as serving dishes—the most special picnic can end up looking like a Tupperware party unless we plan our servingware carefully. Better to wrap the food in foil, then transfer to a serving dish once there.
● Flimsy plastic cups—anywhere, ever, but paper ones curiously are fine.
● Swiss army knives—we're not hiking and they're too small to be of any real use slicing food.
● Plastic picnic tables—we'd rather sit on a blanket even if it does challenge our joints. Or take a colorful cloth to disguise it.
● Campaign picnic chairs with integral drinks holders—we're not watching golf.
● DITTO oversize stripy umbrellas—although if this is your biggest one.....
● An aerosol of fly spray—so tempting.
● Wet wipes—nothing to wash the smell off afterward. Better a thermos of water and a cloth.

PICNIC KIT

HAMPERS AND BASKETS

I like to put together my own hamper depending on what we are eating; those rather formal wicker baskets that come with cutlery strapped to the lid leave me feeling ill at ease. Most usually I opt for a big wicker basket and a stripy beach or other lightweight straw bag. This way we only take what we need. Sometimes the starting point is indeed a hamper, something that on occasions we get given filled with goodies, which are usefully employed thereafter. Wrap everything in linen napkins or dish towels if it is likely to rattle around, and these can be used as cloths to spread the food on.

COOLER BAGS

De rigueur, even if you take a hamper. I favor cooler bags over boxes, which tend to be heavier and more bulky. The best come lined with insulating material, and you can hedge your bets with ice packs. Hard to have too many; a minimum of two if not three good-size ones for an average picnic. Mini bags are also great for cans of drink.

DINNERWARE

The occasional real china item can provide a civilizing note, and if I am taking a plate of food or a tart, then I might transport it on a favorite vintage china plate. Most of my picnic kit consists of bits and bobs that I have amassed at yard sales, or it may be the odds and ends of sets that have subsequently been broken or gotten lost. The result is a friendly mishmash that works together as a whole because the last thing that matters on a picnic is matching plates and cutlery. It is then of little consequence if anything goes missing.

I also love wooden platters, the more distressed the better. There is a big revival in melamine, which is pretty much perfect for picnics, as it is lightweight and unbreakable. But shop with care here as there is melamine and melamine, and the good stuff is something that wouldn't shame us at home. There is plenty of retro melamine on the market that will cut a dash mingling with old china. Lightweight acrylic is also a good material—I particularly like clear tableware that could at a distance stand in for glass.

PLATES

If you go down the proper china route it can get heavy, so this is where I tend to turn to paper or thin ply plates, not least because you can throw them away afterward, so there's no dishwashing involved. But otherwise, enamelware is ever brilliant, and if you camp, it's quite likely you'll have some of this in any case.

CUTLERY

For truly lightweight cutlery, wooden is ideal. And the rather odd-sounding "sporks" that combine spoon at one end with fork at the other do make sense. There is some kitsch but pretty acetate picnic cutlery around too. On the real front, a selection of bone-handled odds and ends is more alluring than stainless steel. You can wrap these items up in a napkin or clean dish towel to transport them, which will double as a small cloth once unwrapped.

GLASSES AND CUPS

I would forego all idea of glasses with stems, as Champagne never tastes better than when drunk out of a tumbler, wine and hard cider ditto. My solution is a mishmash of glasses collected in ones and twos from junk stores and sales. The other very useful type are stainless steel shooting cups, which stack to nothing and are also light.

Or serve your wine in small melamine or Bakelite mugs—baby's or children's ones come in just the right size.

CONTAINERS AND SERVING DISHES

Unless you are traveling a short distance from car to picnic, you will almost certainly want to pack food in an airtight container. The most efficient are Lock & Lock, which are air- and liquid-tight once you have clipped the wings into place (it is Murphy's Law that many of the prettier-colored plastic ones are also least efficient). But you can always juggle here, and use the pretty sort for baked goods, stacking finger foods between layers of parchment paper. Then transport anything likely to spill in a lockable container. Maybe take some lightweight acetate, melamine, or bamboo bowls to transfer the food once you arrive; enameled tin trays make excellent large serving plates too. Stackable sets of plastic containers have the advantage that once empty you can slot them within each other and then pop them in a plastic bag to transport home. Cork is another favorite material, featherlight and rustic. And look out for tiffin carriers, a brilliant system of stacking several different dishes on top of each other, and clamping the stack shut. These come with a carry handle.

The alternative for rustic chic are canning jars, good for sauces and relishes, a drop of milk, or whatever. These could be Le Parfait clip-top jars that come in various sizes, or ones that you have collected over the years. Be sure to hang on to little jam jars that might not make sense in terms of homemade preserves but are ideal for any sauces, condiments, or chopped herbs you want to take. And old-fashioned tins are good for baked treats.

THERMOS

It's worth taking a thermos of chilled water; if not for drinks, it will come in handy for wiping down sticky fingers. Fill with water and lots of ice cubes.

MINUSCULE CUTTING BOARD

The smallest possible cutting board serves for slicing salamis, cheeses, and tomatoes, or cutting the base off a head of lettuce or Belgian endive. The lighter the better—cork or bamboo are ideal.

TRAVELING GRILL

Weber's "Smokey Joe Gold," a miniature charcoal kettle grill with a lid, is a bit bulkier than other portable charcoal types, but if you have the space it's a guarantee of great results. The handle clips over the lid so that you can carry it without any ash falling out, or even move it around once it's lit. Most importantly, avoid disposable grills, but not without taking a leaf out of their book by loading your grill with briquettes and firelighters before you go.

TRASH BAGS

So important, for all those scraps at the end, and the dirty dinnerware. Take at least one large one, and then some small ones too, double-lined unless they are trusted not to leak on the way home.

FOOD BAGS AND TIES

A roll of these also comes in handy for transporting any leftovers back home.

CORKSCREW

If you are transporting the bottles upright, why not open them before you go? Some folding knives also usefully come with one attached, so you can keep it ready in the picnic bag.

SEA SALT AND BLACK PEPPER

Tastes differ, and it's as well to take a bit of seasoning for those that feel they want more. One route is to take a small envelope of the two mixed together, or a pill box. There are also some good travel and picnic designs around.

Knife Hall of Fame

FOLDING KNIVES

The most sophisticated outward-bound folding knives tend to come with a host of attachments that are redundant on a picnic, a corkscrew and bottle opener aside. The most useful folding knives are also some of the most elegant. A single blade is all we are after, but a slightly longer one than normal, some 4½ inches long, which will serve us proud for slicing and cutting.

Opinel: Hard to imagine life without these iconic wooden and steel folding knives, so simple, reliable, and beautifully designed. Still made entirely in France, by the descendants of Jospeh Opinel who designed the original in 1890. It comes in sizes ranging 1 to 12.

A rustic wooden-handled folding knife with a steel blade; the safety ring that locks the blade both open or closed was added at a later date. One of the cheapest solutions around, my choice is to give one to every diner when knives and forks are called for, as well as relying on them for slicing cheese, cake, and the like.

Laguiole: I have a complete passion for these exquisite handmade folding knives. They are something to treasure for a lifetime, and I often give them as Christening or milestone gifts. But beware of fakes—these must be one of the most copied articles outside of Gucci bags, as sadly the original artisanal producers failed to patent their design in time. Today there are just a handful of traditional forges making the knives.

The humble beginnings of the Laguiole knife go back to the early nineteenth century, to the village of the same name, home to an array of isolated farms. In the winter months, the family elders would migrate to Catalonia to work as sawyers, returning with a Spanish "navaja" knife. The slender handle and yatagan-shape blade of today's Laguiole took inspiration from these knives, which provided a blueprint.

There are any number of fascinating stories surrounding Laguiole knives that can be found on www.layole.com, the house of "Honoré Durand," one of the best and very few artisanal forges. It is only recently that the tradition for artisanal production has once again established itself locally, having been eclipsed for decades by the mechanized industrial production at Thiers. The real thing involves some 109 different stages of craftsmanship, and the knife will come with a certificate of authenticity. A bee on the handle and the word Laguiole on the blade is not enough!

LamsonSharp Batard: This king-size folding picnic knife (with corkscrew) was designed by Charles van Over, author of *The Best Bread Ever*, who insists that bread should be cut properly. But finding a serrated bread knife to take on a picnic all but impossible, he persuaded the U.S. manufacturers Lamson and Goodnow to team up and they produced this. Its use goes far beyond just bread.

KNIVES WITH GUARDS

Wusthof Trident: If you don't want to invest in special picnicware, my favorite range of kitchen knives by Wusthof Trident also comes with knife guards. The Classic 6¼-inch serrated sausage knife has long been my desert island choice. Just big enough for slicing a loaf of bread, it makes short work of tomatoes, salamis, or a roast.

Kuhn Rikon: These razor-sharp pop-colored knives with protective shields deserve to become a modern classic. Designed for the Swiss manufacturer Kuhn Rikon by Philipp Beyeler, they come in a picnic-perfect range of bright jelly hues, with or without polka dots, gingham, and the like. Their Japanese carbon steel blades defy the innocence of their appearance. And they're affordable.

Lounging

BLANKETS

For any more than two people, a couple of picnic blankets (or more) make sense and allow for spreading the picnic out and lazing full length at the same time. If the weather is dry, then a plastic back doesn't really matter, although a heavy dew can leave the ground feeling damp for the best part of the day, so it's good to have at least one waterproof option up your sleeve. Thick woollen blankets are still a personal favorite, and these can also be found with plastic backs. Lightweight blankets that you can fold down to nothing are again extremely useful.

CLOTHS

If you only have one blanket, then use this for sitting on and spread out a cloth for the food. Lovely new linen dish towels make great picnic cloths, anything jazzy that seems far too good to dry up with. Old-fashioned tray cloths are also a good size. Another option if the weather is dry is a thick linen-effect disposable cloth.

FLEECES

I like to take a warm fleece blanket, for that extra comfort, and many is the time it has doubled as a blanket when the chill sets in.

CUSHIONS

Nothing special here, just something small and light that you won't mind getting dirty, and/or wet.

PICNIC TABLES AND CHAIRS

There is a wonderful display in the Musée de la Chasse et de la Nature in Paris, France of a hunting picnic, with a low coffee-table-height table and cushions around it, by which all others will be judged. But finding such a table is most likely to involve cutting down an inexpensive folding table to the required height.

Fishing stools make the simplest of chairs to perch on. Trawl eBay and you might even find them with a table, a neat arrangement where they slot inside the base of the table.

PICNIC LIGHTS

Solar outdoor lights have revolutionized the dusk or evening picnic. Folding Chinese lanterns and strings of lights are perfect for hanging in trees. Otherwise some tealights in small jars will cast the right kind of magic, as well as being protected from the wind.

WASP DETERRENT

For the wasp- (and hornet/yellowjacket) phobe, of which I am one, it doesn't take more than a couple of the determined little creatures to send you back indoors. There is no rationale behind the hatred of these insects, but were a wasp to position itself between me and a pile of priceless china in a store, I could do more damage than a bull. So a couple of "waspinators" is a brilliant defense for the picknicker. These ingenious devices mimic a wasp nest, deterring the insects, which are territorial by nature, making them think they are likely to be attacked if they go any closer. Lightweight and transportable, just hang a couple within the vicinity of the picnic and hope the wasps are sufficiently gullible.

"Tealights in small jars will cast the right kind of magic, as well as being protected from the wind."

A CHECKLIST FOR PICNIC PERFECTION

I have a checklist pinned inside a kitchen cabinet door for what to pack on vacation that still reads "baby bottles," "drinking cup," and "changing pad," even though my youngest son is now a teenager. But it also has things like "passport," "cell phone," "euros," and "house key," and I have to say it does the trick. You may not need everything itemized on the list below, but run through it before you leave and it just might save you having to drive back home to get the picnic bag, corkscrew, or similar. We've all done that.

The Picnic list

The picnic food itself

Glasses

Mugs

Plates—eating and serving

Knives, forks, spoons

Folding knife

Corkscrew

Salt and pepper

Napkins

Small bread board

Dish towels

Tablecloth clips

Food cover

Waspinator

Thermos

Cold drinks

Hot drinks

If barbecuing:

Grill preloaded with briquettes and firelighters

Matches

Tongs

Sturdy plate or tray for the hot food

Paraphernalia

Sun hats

Sunscreen

Sunglasses

Umbrella

Waterproof

Picnic blankets

Fleece

Cushions

Stools or chairs

Picnic table

Paper towels

Plastic wrap

Big and small plastic bags for leftovers

Games

RECIPE SYMBOLS GUIDE

These symbols appear next to the following recipes as a guide to enable you to easily match recipes to your picnic.

COMMUNAL
good to pass around when there are lots of people

GLAMOROUS
special-occasion picnics

IN ADVANCE
can be made in advance of the day of the picnic

E ADDRESS BOOK

eBay for vintage picnic kit.

www.lakeland.co.uk for the best lightweight cooler bags (their own brand), lined with flectalon, which works like a thermos. This reflective silvered material was originally developed for NASA astronauts in space. The food remains at the same temperature as when it is put into the bag, even when left in the sun. Two or three of these, which will pack inside each other when not in use, revolutionize outdoor eating. Lakeland also offer a great range of picnic kit in season, including lovely paper plates and napkins, acrylicware, and practical solutions such as food covers. Ships to the US.

www.emmabridgewater.co.uk for sturdy, beautifully made and designed melamine. As well as her plates, the baby mugs make quirky wine glasses. Her enameled tins are also excellent, and her trays double as unbreakable serving dishes, great for passing a big plate of anything around. Free shipping to the US.

www.layole.com One of the last-remaining authentic forges making Laguiole knives. Have these customized to order with the handle, blade length, and attachments of your choice, and your initials. Slicing a salami or hunk of cheese doesn't get more luxurious.

www.roullierwhite.com This elegant online living emporium tempts on any number of fronts, but seek out the Batard folding picnic knife.

www.inthehaus.co.uk for classic Wusthof knives with guards. Available on amazon.com or macys.com.

www.kuhnrikon.com for razor-sharp colorful plastic picnic knives with protective guards.

www.notonthehighstreet.com This marketplace of small quirky companies makes a brilliant hunting ground for picnic blankets, bags, plastic containers, and other useful outdoor accoutrement.

www.josephjoseph.com If the talented brothers who run this kitchen design business can't solve the problem, no one can. Their designs are modern classics, and we want a whole range on our picnics—their grip tray, their salad servers, salad bowl with a carry-handle built into the rim, their two-in-one salt and pepper grinder, the list goes on and on.

www.bambuhome.com for eco-friendly "Bambu" veneer picnicware and lightweight lacquered bamboo bowls in jazzy colors.

www.surplusandoutdoors.com for classic enamelware, which will double as camping gear.

www.target.com for our favorite stackable sets of Lock & Lock containers, which are the original and still the best of their kind.

www.weber.com for the bijoux traveling "Smokey Joe" grills in this season's colors.

www.amazon.com for Thermos Work Series steel thermoses that will keep food hot or cold for 24 hours, and Thermos multipurpose food and drink thermoses that come with an option of pourers— good for soup, oatmeal, and the like. Also for Waspinators, an environment-friendly solution to these hungry little pests. A couple of these mock nests fold up to nothing; hang them nearby and hope the resident wasps are fooled.

www.ikea-usa.com will have a great range of inexpensive and well-designed picnic gear during any summer. We especially love their solar lanterns.

us.marimekko.com for gorgeous bright textiles that are perfect on picnics. I love their big tea towels, as well as their tablecloths. They also have great canvas carry-alls.

www.picnicbaskets.com for every kind of picnic basket, blanket and accessorie—wine tray, travel grill, tub cooler etc— the way to do it in style!

www.atlanticblankets.com for luxurious, thick, traditional woollen blankets and picnic blankets in up-to-the-minute designs.

www.tartanrugs.com for good-quality waterproof-backed picnic blankets.

www.zoeppritz.com for the softest, warmest fleece blankets in fab jewel-like colors, seek out this long-established German manufacturer.

www.jaquesamerica.com for the most beautiful outdoor games, be it boules in a wooden box, or the chic volleyball and rounders sets in their familiar dark green canvas cases. These come perfectly packaged and designed for the picknicker who likes to play.

DIPS, PÂTÉS & COLD CUTS

It is the prospect of feasting that

gets so many of us pulling out the hamper, the sheer plenty that goes hand in hand with the occasion. As a guest, trying to guess what lies within the cook's box of tricks makes for a tantalizing game, as appetites are whetted by all that fresh air. The legendary exchange between Rat and Mole in Kenneth Grahame's *The Wind in the Willows* encapsulates it so perfectly, when in answer to Mole's wiggling curiosity of what is inside the wicker basket, Rat replies: "There's cold chicken inside it…coldtonguecold-hamcoldbeefpickledgherkinssaladfrenchrolls-cresssandwichespottedmeatgingerbeerlemon-adesodawater."

You don't have to unravel it (or be British) to get the point. It is almost worth lugging one of those heavy and wholly impractical hampers across a few fields for nothing more than the excitement of seeing a laden case, groaning with goodies, set down on the grass and others wondering what could possibly lie within.

Well, for starters, cold meats, pâtés, and little pots of deliciousness, we hope. Dipping and spreading are a large part of any relaxed picnic, a DIY bar for grazing with plentiful crudités, breads, and pickles. There are lots of instant solutions: ready-made dips that can be jazzed up in a jiffy as a cheat's take on the real thing. In fact, I felt slightly mortified recently on a picnic when my cheating dips seemed to attract more praise than anything else. But having repackaged them in attractive containers, I guess I asked for it.

For a slightly more soignée occasion, then a whole ham or some home-cured gravlax (see page 45) are both readily accessible, can be made well in advance, and will be streets ahead of anything that comes sliced and plastic-wrapped. One of the most enchanting picnics I have been on recently (or ever, in fact) was a dîner en blanc. I had never heard of these until I found myself in a communal garden dressed top to toe in white along with a couple of hundred other people dressed in a similar fashion, tables bedecked in white linen, with vases of white flowers and hundreds of white candles, lit as the sun was sinking (see page 39).

We shouldn't be too surprised to learn that dîner en blanc emanates from Paris, France, capital of chic, and they have actually been around for several decades. Just pop the search term dîner en blanc into Google images and you'll be met with a wonderful array of snaps, such as the one where some ten thousand picnickers took over the Place de la Concorde, all at fifteen minutes' notice of its whereabouts in order to foil any niggling authorities. It's the extreme in flash-mob dining, a massive Chinese whisper that starts doing the rounds courtesy of Twitter or a few well-placed texts to the right friends.

By comparison, we had plenty of warning for the one I attended—well, the luxury of twenty-four hours I seem to remember, though for a Londoner with a busy diary this still seemed on the racy side of spontaneous. And going back to where I started, the first course was so beautifully simple and right for the occasion: a large baked ham and equally large piece of Parmesan laid out on a trestle table with its own white linen cloth.

"It's worth lugging one of those heavy hampers across a few fields for the excitement of seeing a laden case, groaning with goodies."

LET'S GO: DIPS

We love damning convenience foods, but where would most of us be without those plastic tubs of hummus, guacamole, and so on. A lot of it isn't bad at all, but that small homemade touch injects an essential element of nurture. In pretty much every case there are invariably one or two finishes that will bring out the best in the dip. Or, you could go further, as it takes little longer to whip up a creamy dip using sour cream or Greek yogurt. Rustle up some crudités and olives and you are well on your way to a respectable feast of a picnic.

HUMMUS

Stir ½ teaspoon of ground **cumin** into a 10-ounce tub of **hummus**. Transfer this to a portable container or bowl, drizzle over a bit of **extra virgin olive oil** and a squeeze of **lemon juice**, and dust with a bit more cumin.
For 4 to 6 people

GUACAMOLE

Stir 2 teaspoons of finely chopped **cilantro leaves** into an 8-ounce tub of **guacamole**. Transfer to a portable container or bowl, drizzle over some **extra virgin olive oil**, dust with **cayenne pepper**, and scatter over a bit more cilantro.
For 4 people

TARAMASALATA

Stir ½ teaspoon of finely grated **lemon zest** and a tablespoon of finely chopped **parsley** into an 8-ounce jar or tub of **taramasalata**. Transfer to a portable container or bowl, drizzle over a bit of **extra virgin olive oil** and a squeeze of **lemon juice**, and scatter over some more parsley.
For 4 people

TZATZIKI

Stir 1 teaspoon of **extra virgin olive oil** and 2 teaspoons of finely chopped **mint** into an 8-ounce tub of **tzatziki**. Transfer to a portable container or a bowl, drizzle over some more oil, and scatter over a few tiny mint leaves.
For 4 people

CHEAT'S AIOLI

The short cut to making an aioli uses sour cream instead of mayonnaise. It makes for an elegant dip, as well as a sauce that can be slathered over food from the grill or cold roasted beef (see page 115).

In a bowl, beat 1⅓ cups **sour cream** with 2 peeled and crushed **garlic cloves**, ½ tablespoon of **lemon juice**, and a bit of **sea salt**. Spoon into a clean bowl or container. Cover and chill until required. Before you leave the house, dust the top with **Piment d'Espelette or cayenne pepper**.
For 8 to 10 people

CREAMED GOAT CHEESE

This creamy dip can be tinkered with endlessly, using different ingredients and flavorings depending on what you want to serve it with, but roasted vegetables are always a good starting point, as is a bowl of feisty green leaves with a walnut dressing.

In a food processor, process 9 ounces **fresh young goat cheese** with ⅓ heaping cup **Greek-style yogurt or fromage blanc** and ⅓ heaping cup **crème fraîche** until creamy. It will probably be slightly grainy, but that's fine. Transfer to a bowl and stir in 2 tablespoons of finely snipped **chives**. Cover and chill until required. Before you leave for the picnic, dust the top with **paprika**.
For 6 people

LABNA

This light, herbed cream cheese is no more arduous to prepare than the preceding instantly drummed-up dips, except that this one needs to be left overnight. Delicious with bresaola, coppa, échine de porc séchée, and other such delicate cured meats.

For 4 to 6 people

2 cups Greek-style yogurt
1 tablespoon each of finely chopped mint, chives, and flat-leaf parsley
½ teaspoon sea salt
cayenne pepper or Piment d'Espelette, for dusting

In a bowl, beat the yogurt with the herbs and salt. Transfer to a fine-mesh strainer (or one lined with a clean dish towel) set over a large bowl and chill for 24 hours. Spoon what remains in the strainer or dish towel into a bowl or container and smooth the surface. Dust with cayenne pepper or Piment d'Espelette before leaving.

Kit Serving spoon, plate, table knife

DUCK RILLETTES

Rillettes rely on meat that is cooked for so long that it gives up all resistance and falls into succulent shreds at the pressure of a fork. This is a cheat's take.

For 6 to 8 people

1 large jar or can confit of duck or goose, at room temperature (containing 26 ounces meat, approx. 14 ounces shredded weight)
a pinch each of ground cinnamon, cloves, nutmeg, and allspice
1 tablespoon thyme leaves
3 tablespoons Cointreau or Grand Marnier
sea salt and black pepper

In a medium saucepan, gently heat the confit through, about 10 minutes, turning the meat halfway through. Transfer it to a plate and take it off the bone, discarding any fat. Shred it using two forks and transfer to a large bowl. Add the spices and thyme.

Strain the fat and drippings into a bowl and measure out ¾ heaping cup fat. Assuming the confit had a pool of jellied drippings in the bottom, pour these into a small saucepan, add the liqueur, and simmer to reduce to a couple of tablespoons of sticky glaze. Mix these into the shredded meat, then add the reserved fat and season to taste.

Pack the mixture into a 0.5-liter Le Parfait canning jar, pressing the mixture down well to exclude any air bubbles. Cover and chill. It will keep for a couple of weeks.

Kit Plate, table knife

POTTED HAM WITH CORNICHONS

This is one step on from sliced roasted ham that not only passes the travel test with flying colors but conveniently comes with the butter and relish all in. Something in the way of crudités, such as celery hearts, and a hearty chunk of bread and you are done. You can pack it into a big dish for communal appreciation, or into individual pots or ramekins for a more glamorous affair.

For 6 people

1 to 1$^1/_3$ cups unsalted butter
1 heaping teaspoon whole grain mustard
14 ounces baked ham, fat removed and diced
$^1/_3$ cup sliced baby cornichons
4 tablespoons coarsely chopped flat-leaf parsley, plus extra leaves to decorate

In a large skillet, heat 7 tablespoons of the butter over lowish heat and stir in the mustard. Add the ham, then fold in the cornichons and parsley.

Pack the mixture either into six 5- or 6-ounce ramekins or into a larger dish or two, pressing it down well, and wipe the rims with paper towels. Cover with plastic wrap and chill until the butter sets, 1 to 2 hours.

Decorate the ramekins or dishes with parsley leaves. In a small saucepan, melt the remaining butter (the amount you will need will depend on the surface area to be sealed; shallow dishes will call for more than deep ones), skim off the surface foam, and pour the clear butter over the top of the parsley (discarding the milky residue at the bottom), pressing the leaves down to submerge them. Chill until set, another 1 to 2 hours, then cover.

Kit Serving spoon, plate, table knife

FARMHOUSE CHICKEN LIVER PÂTÉ

This silky pâté is a staple in our house and it freezes well, so it's a good one for that getting-ready-in-advance picnic. Dish it up with some chutney, radishes, gherkins, and pickled onions and some grainy brown bread, and all you need are a couple of cheeses in addition. It's unusual to come across fresh chicken livers, so look out for them in the frozen-foods section.

For 4 to 6 people

1 cup (2 sticks) unsalted butter
8 ounces chicken livers, fatty membranes removed
1 bay leaf
2 thyme sprigs
sea salt and black pepper

1 shallot, peeled and finely chopped
1 garlic clove, peeled and finely chopped
2 tablespoons Calvados or brandy
1 tablespoon crème fraîche
freshly grated nutmeg

In a large skillet, melt 2 tablespoons of the butter over medium heat. When the foam starts to subside, add the chicken livers and the herbs, season, and sauté until the livers are golden on the outside but still pink in the centre, 3 minutes, turning them halfway through cooking. Discard the herbs and add the livers with any drippings to a blender.

Add another pat of butter to the pan and fry the shallot and garlic until glossy and translucent, about 2 minutes. Add the Calvados or brandy to the pan and simmer until it has all but disappeared. Transfer the contents of the pan to the blender and purée with the crème fraîche.

Let cool for about 20 minutes, then dice and add the remaining butter and beat until the pâté is really smooth and creamy. Add a grating of nutmeg and adjust the seasoning. (I like to pass the pâté through a fine strainer to ensure it's as silky as possible, but you don't have to.)

Spoon the pâté into a jar or a bowl, smooth the surface, cover, and chill until required. It keeps well for at least 48 hours in the fridge.

Kit Plate, table knife

POTTED CRAB

Like miniature shrimp, crab makes a delicious buttery pâté for piling on a crust of bread, with a few salad greens or radishes in attendance. In fact, this picnic treat is one of the best uses for crab that I can think of, where the brown meat is as readily employed as the white. Just find a grassy dune or a hillock with a good view of the sea to enhance it.

For 6 people

²/₃ cup unsalted butter
13 ounces fresh white and brown crabmeat,
   picked over for shells and cartilage
juice of ½ lemon
¹/₃ teaspoon ground mace
¹/₃ teaspoon cayenne pepper
sea salt
1 bay leaf

In a small skillet, melt 7 tablespoons of the butter over medium heat, add the crabmeat, and stir until heated through. Add the lemon juice, mace, cayenne pepper, and a bit of salt to taste. Pack into a bowl, cover, and chill until it firms, about an hour. In a small saucepan, melt the remaining butter, lay a bay leaf over the surface of the crab, and pour over the butter. Cover and chill. This will keep well for a couple of days in the fridge.

Kit Plate, table knife

POTTED SMOKED SALMON WITH LEMON

That little bit more luxurious than a pâté. Smoked salmon always welcomes a few drops of fresh lemon juice at the last minute. I've always loved those lemon halves wrapped in cheesecloth that are the domain of seafood bars, but also a good ruse on a picnic, tied at the pointed end with thin string or white ribbon. Failing a rich curd cheese, you could use ¾ cup whole fromage blanc seasoned with salt and pepper mixed with a heaping tablespoon of thick heavy cream.

For 6 people

7 ounces rich curd cheese or quark
1 teaspoon finely grated lemon zest*
a generous pinch of ground mace
a couple of shakes of Tabasco
14 ounces smoked salmon, brown meat
   cut out, diced
2 tablespoons small capers, rinsed and
   patted dry
2 tablespoons finely chopped chives

In a large bowl, beat together the cheese, lemon zest, mace, and Tabasco, then fold in the smoked salmon. Pack into six little pots or a larger bowl, and wipe the rims with paper towels. Scatter over the capers and chives, though save doing this until the morning of the picnic if making these more than a day in advance, and chill. They will keep for several days in the fridge.

Kit Plate, table knife

*Tip Use a grater not a zester here.

MACKEREL RILLETTES

Mackerel is a deliciously succulent and moist fish, and combining fresh with the smoked version gives you the best of both worlds. Here, rillettes make a virtuously healthy pâté, with lots of fish oils boosted by some extra virgin olive oil. I'd dish this up with some crisp croutons (see page 53), and perhaps some radishes and gherkins.

For 6 people

10½ to 14 ounces fresh mackerel fillets (approx. 21 to 25 ounces whole fish)
10½ ounces smoked mackerel fillets
2 bay leaves
3 garlic cloves, peeled and halved lengthwise
black pepper
1/3 heaping cup white wine
3 tablespoons water
a squeeze of lemon juice
3 tablespoons extra virgin olive oil
2 scallions, trimmed and finely sliced
sea salt

Arrange the fresh and smoked mackerel fillets over the bottom of a large saucepan. Add the bay leaves and garlic and grind over some black pepper. Pour over the wine and the water and bring to a boil, then cover and cook for 2 minutes over medium heat. Remove from the heat and let cool for several hours.

Pour the liquid into a small saucepan and simmer to reduce to a couple of tablespoons of liquid in total. Flake the fish into a bowl, discarding any bones and skin, including the tough surface skin on the smoked fillets. Pour over the reduced liquid, a squeeze of lemon juice, and 2 tablespoons of olive oil, and gently mix in two thirds of the scallions, trying not to break up the flakes. Taste and add a bit of salt if you think it needs it.

Transfer the rillettes to a clean bowl or jar with an airtight lid and chill. Drizzle over another tablespoon of oil and scatter over the remaining scallions before setting off for your picnic.

Kit Serving spoon, plate, table knife

MAPLE BAKED HAM

Baked hams make as much of a star turn at a picnic as they do on the Thanksgiving or Christmas table, be it at that dîner en blanc (see page 39), or any other occasion when you are trying to cater for eight or ten friends and want something wholly practical but rather special too.

Should you be any more in number, then you could roast a couple of chickens or buy a round of Brie or another gooey cheese. It is worth checking when buying the ham whether or not it needs soaking overnight. Mostly a change of water in the process of cooking will do the trick.

For 6 to 8 people

One 4½-pound boneless uncooked cured
  half ham
3 outer celery stalks, trimmed and sliced
2 carrots, trimmed and sliced
1 leek, trimmed and sliced
2 bay leaves
2 tablespoons maple syrup
1 teaspoon molasses
2 teaspoons English mustard

Place the ham in a large saucepan (I use a jam pan), cover with cold water, and bring to a boil. Discard the water and start again with fresh water to cover, this time adding the chopped vegetables and bay leaves. Bring to a boil, then maintain at a gentle simmer over low heat for 50 minutes. If necessary, top up with boiling water halfway through.

Heat the oven to 400°F. Transfer the ham from the saucepan onto a board using two forks (the broth makes excellent soup, though it may need reducing). Remove any string around the ham and pull off the rind. Slice the fat at ¾-inch intervals with a crisscross pattern without cutting down to the flesh.

In a bowl, combine the maple syrup, molasses, and mustard. Use this to coat the ham evenly all over. If you like you can also tie another couple of pieces of string around the ham if it seems loose. Place the ham in a roasting pan and pour about ½ inch of the ham broth into the base to prevent any syrup that trickles down from burning. Bake for 35 to 45 minutes, until the glaze is mahogany-colored and dry. Let the ham cool. If you carve it at home before setting off, wrap it up tightly in foil to transport.

Kit Plate, serving fork

GRAVLAX

Passionate as I am about cooking, I tend to draw the line at home-smoking and making bread. Gravlax, however, is the easiest cured fish to prepare and enormously satisfying to make. And, most importantly, you can guarantee the quality of your salmon in the first place, something that gets harder and harder when you buy packaged and sliced cured salmon. The ideal section is from the thickest part of a whole fish—ask for it to be filleted into two pieces, leaving the skin on, but don't fret if it turns out differently. This is a good dish to freeze, even presliced, and makes an elegant centerpiece. Lovely laid on a slice of buttered soda or rye bread, but equally delicious on a small crisp lettuce leaf.

For 6 to 8 people

2/3 cup coarse sea salt
1/2 cup superfine sugar
2 tablespoons yellow mustard seeds
a small bunch of dill or chervil (approx.
   3/4 ounce), finely chopped, plus 2 tablespoons
   to serve
2 pounds salmon fillet, skin-on, pin bones
   removed
Boston lettuce heart leaves or buttered soda
   or rye bread, to serve

MUSTARD SAUCE

In a bowl, whisk together 2/3 cup **sour cream**, 1 heaping tablespoon **Dijon mustard**, 1 heaping tablespoon **whole grain mustard**, 1 scant tablespoon **superfine sugar**. Let stand for 10 minutes to allow the sugar to dissolve, then stir again. Cover and chill until required.

In a bowl, combine the salt, sugar, mustard seeds, and dill or chervil. Scatter a quarter of the salt mixture over a piece of plastic wrap large enough to wrap the two fillets up in when placed on top of each other. Place one fillet skin-down on top, scatter over two thirds of the remaining mixture, then lay the second fillet on top so that the thick part of the fillet is on top of the thin part of the fillet, and they lie flesh to flesh. Scatter over the remaining salt mixture, wrap the salmon up, and then in foil.

Two heavy cast-iron roasting pans that fit inside each other provide the best route to curing and weighting the fish. Place the salmon inside the larger dish and place the smaller dish on top (anything lighter will require weighting with a can or two). Chill for 48 hours, turning the parcel every 12 hours. During this time the sugar and salt will draw the juices out of the salmon and turn into a sticky brine.

Unwrap the salmon and rinse the marinade off the flesh side. Some of the mustard seeds and dill should remain but you will get rid of the excess salt and sugar. Place the fillets skin-down on the work surface, then place a paper towel over each fillet and press to absorb any excess liquid, and repeat. Press the 2 tablespoons of finely chopped dill or chervil into the surface.

Trim the edge of the fillets if very thin, then slice the gravlax diagonally off the skin, thicker than you would smoked salmon, discarding the ends. Serve with some mustard sauce.

Kit Spoon, plate

BREADS, TARTS & PIES

We seem to spend a great deal of

our time planning for the future instead of living in the present. And perhaps this is one reason why so often spontaneous last-minute picnics prove the most magical. They come as a lovely surprise that you haven't factored into your jam-packed diary, until you happen to wake up to a crystal-clear blue sky on a weekend morning and think, why not, let's go.

One reason why not, I suppose, is children, and if I am honest I think I did more of this before having a family, but I still cling to the idyll. Especially when I think back to one rather perfect lunch when we took off to a water-meadow just outside Henley, Oxfordshire in the English countryside, and parked ourselves with a posse of friends on a thin strip of land hemmed in by a field of rapeseed in full flower on one side and by the River Thames on the other, with the enchanting folly Temple Island in the middle. To this day I can recall the luminous yellow of the oilseed rape (I have looked fondly on this crop ever since) set against the bottomless blue of the sky. There was an alluring faint chill in the air befitting the entrance to the Chiltern Hills visible in the distance.

The starting point for almost any such opportunism is good bread. Now as one of life's freezer-phobes, bread is an exception and one of the few items that I do keep frozen. Good bread is hard to find, so I buy a loaf or two whenever I happen to chance across it. It thaws in no time. You don't even need to plan as far as the night before—a couple of hours at an ambient temperature and it should be deliciously soft and fresh.

And then, of course, you want lots of lovely bits and pieces to adorn its crumb. You may well have some of the essentials—I'm thinking olives and soft sundried tomatoes, maybe some onions in balsamic vinegar, pickled chiles, and a jar of artichokes in oil—that you can call on. Then again you may not, in which case it's a quick trip to the grocery store. So all that's left is the need for cheese and cold cuts, and again, given these are keepers, you may be able to pad out with what you have on hand. Canned sardines in chile oil are a staple of my pantry, gorgeous with a crust of bread and ripe tomatoes. It could be that simple.

"Good bread is hard to find, so I buy a loaf or two whenever I happen to chance across it."

LET'S GO: DIY SANDWICH BAR

What follows is really a reminder of the sort of goodies that are ripe for assembling a DIY sandwich bar once you get there. The only possible guideline is perhaps to think of grouping ingredients with the same geographical leanings together: for instance, fill focaccia with tapenade, goat cheese, artichokes in oil, roasted bell peppers, and arugula; or pile corned beef, gherkins, and sauerkraut onto buttered rye; marry Black Forest ham with smoked cheese. However you play it, the idea is zero preparation; just pack and go.

BREADS
Baguettes, sourdough loaves, rye bread, focaccia and petit pains, crusty whole grain loaves, finger rolls, and carta di musica.

SPREADS
Tapenade, hummus (see page 30), taramasalata (see page 30), sundried tomato paste, pesto, cream cheese, and mayonnaise.

SUNDRIES
Sundried tomatoes in oil, pitted green and black olives, artichokes in oil, roasted red bell peppers in oil, caper berries, pickled chiles, grilled/charbroiled zucchini, salted anchovies, crab, smoked cod or carp roe (tarama), cooked peeled shrimp, cocktail gherkins, and sauerkraut.

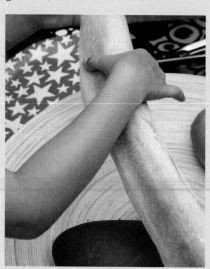

CHUTNEYS
Cranberry sauce, apricot chutney, and sweet tomato and chile relish (see page 58).

SALAD
Arugula, watercress, garden cress, flat-leaf parsley, baby leaves, salad sprouts, basil, cucumber, radishes, and cherry tomatoes.

COLD CUTS
Air-dried ham, baked ham, salami, mortadella, corned beef, and pastrami.

CHEESES
Feta, Parmesan slivers, buffalo mozzarella, Roquefort, Fourme d'Ambert, Gouda, Cantal, Gruyère, Brie, Gorgonzola, Manchego, cheddar, and Lancashire.

PICNIC REUBENS
This classic German sandwich, championed by New Yorkers, is usually served hot, but makes a great picnic dish too. Pile **buttered rye bread** with fine slivers of **Gruyère or Comté**, **sauerkraut**, **pastrami**, and **Russian dressing** (3 heaping tablespoons **mayonnaise**, 1 heaping tablespoon **ketchup**, 1 heaping teaspoon **horseradish sauce**, ½ teaspoon **Worcestershire sauce**).

PROPER CROUTONS

It is one thing to plunder the dank interior of a good cheese shop, and ask at your local gourmet market for the slicer to be on its finest setting for that haunch of air-dried ham on display. But good croutons? Even the very French neighborhood patisserie is likely to fail on this one, and there is nothing quite like them for scooping up a gooey Gorgonzola or Brie de Meaux, or a spoon of silky chicken liver pâté (see page 37). Deliciously crisp and delicate, you want a refined baguette here rather than a "baguette de tradition" or sourdough type. These can be rustled up a day or two in advance of a picnic.

Preheat the oven to 400°F. Slice a slim **baguette** about ¼ inch thick for slim croutons, or ½ inch thick for more robust ones. Lay them out on cookie sheets and toast in the oven until they have dried out, 5 minutes. Paint each side with **olive oil** and return to the oven for another 5 to 8 minutes, depending on their thickness, or until they are golden-brown and crisp. Let cool before transferring to a plastic food bag or container.

CRUSTY GARLIC OLIVE BREAD

This picnic loaf has garlic-bread-like charm, soaked in olive oil infused with garlic, with olives and also herbs for good measure.

Makes 1 small baton or ½ baguette

Whisk 4 tablespoons **extra virgin olive oil** together with 1 crushed **garlic clove,** 2 tablespoons finely chopped **green or black olives,** and 1 tablespoon of **lemon thyme leaves**. Halve a **small baton or half a baguette** lengthwise, leaving the halves attached at the side, and open it out. Drizzle the mixture over the two cut surfaces, spreading the olives out evenly, then wrap it up in foil.

Bake for 15 minutes at 400°F, turning it over halfway through if you remember. Leave it wrapped in foil for easy transporting—it will still be delicious at an ambient temperature.

BREAD AND TOMATOES

I have an enduring love of tomatoes with bread in pretty much every form, from an Italian soup to the English breakfast treat of warm soft, broiled tomatoes mashed into a slice of buttered toast.

Lovely ripe heirloom varieties are one of summer's gifts. Pack up a few carefully chosen specimens and a hearty loaf of bread, with an elegant Sicilian or Provençal extra virgin olive oil and a coarse sea salt, and you have one of life's great rustic picnics. Take it one step further and you can whip up a tray of Majorcan "pa amb oli" or bruschettas, for passing around.

PA AMB OLI

Like bruschettas in Italy, "pa amb oli" is symbolic of Majorcan food. This particular take on bread and tomatoes captures the spirit of this small island in the Mediterranean. Traditional Majorcan bread is neither white nor brown but somewhere in between, does not contain salt, and uses natural leavening. In character it is close-grained and relatively dry, so a rye bread or a light whole wheat are ideal substitutes. I like to make this using the lower half of a slipper-shaped loaf of rye and cut it thickly into fingers. It will lap up almost any amount of olive oil, so it's worth taking an extra small bottle to the picnic to give it a final dousing before passing them around.

For 4 people

Heat a ridged grill pan over high heat and toast the bottom half of a long loaf of **rye bread** or **light whole wheat**, (cut ¾ to 1¼ inches deep) either side, pressing down with a spatula until it brands with stripes—if necessary trim the ends so that it fits. Give the crumb side a few halfhearted swipes with a peeled **garlic clove**, and coat with a dash or two of **extra virgin olive oil**. Your **tomatoes** (you will need a couple of large, juicy plum tomatoes or maybe three smaller ones) should be ripe to the point of bursting. If they haven't already done so, use a knife to make an incision and break them open using your fingers, working over the toast. Squeeze the seeds over the crumb, then mash the flesh onto the surface and throw away the skin and core. Crumble over a few flakes of **sea salt** and splash over a bit more oil. Cut diagonally into 1¼-inch-wide strips and arrange on a plate. These will be good for at least a couple of hours. Splash over a bit more oil before serving.

TOMATO AND ANCHOVY PAN BAGNAT

Another play on bread and tomatoes, this time super-sweet slowly roasted cocktail tomatoes fill a hollowed-out loaf of bread, along with some anchovy fillets and arugula.

For 4 to 6 people

One 14-ounce sourdough loaf
3 tablespoons extra virgin olive oil
10½ ounces slow-roast tomatoes
   (see page 95)
1½ cups arugula
10 salted anchovy fillets

Cut off the top third of the loaf to create a lid, and pull out the inside crumb from both the base and the lid, to leave a shell about ½ inch thick. The insides can be blitzed in a food processor to use as bread crumbs and popped into the freezer.

Drizzle the oil over the cut surfaces, including the rim of both halves, spreading it evenly with a spoon. Spoon two thirds of the tomatoes into the base, lay half the arugula on top, then the anchovies, and then the remaining arugula. Spoon the remaining tomatoes into the lid, then carefully replace this. Wrap the loaf up snugly in plastic wrap, place in a baking dish, and place another lightweight dish on top with either a can or a jar—you want the loaf to be firm enough to slice without actually squashing it. Chill for a couple of hours.

Kit Serrated knife, plate

BRUSCHETTA

I remember driving through the Tuscan hills on our way to Montepulciano in Italy, when we chanced upon a hilltop café that had a large tray of bruschettas on the counter, but bought and consumed in the corner of a Tuscan field, invisibly laced with genius loci, I have been striving to recapture the magic of those tomatoes on toast ever since. In its basic incarnation bruschetta is a soggy affair of overripe tomatoes and lots of very green olive oil (green both in color and in flavor), absorbed by a sturdy slice of toasted white bread. A French "pain de campagne" is probably the most widely available crumb that suits, or a sourdough, but I'd avoid the poor overexposed ciabatta.

For 4 people

Toast four thick slices of **coarsely textured white bread** and, depending on whether it feels sufficiently summery, give it a few halfhearted swipes with a peeled **garlic clove**—be very pathetic about this; a hint of garlic is fine but nothing too boisterous. Place the toast on a plate and coat with a dash or two of **extra virgin olive oil**. Your **tomatoes** (about four) should be ripe to the point of bursting at the seams. If they haven't already done so, use a knife to make an incision and break them open with your fingers, working over the toast.

Squeeze out the seeds—one of best bits of the tomato that fashion would have us discard—then mash the flesh onto the surface and throw away the skin and core. Crumble over a few flakes of **sea salt**. These will be good for at least a couple of hours. Splash over a bit more oil before serving.

BREAD AND CHEESE

There's hardly a nation that doesn't have a contribution to make here, skirting the dairy-free zones of Asia, we can pretty much travel the world on a buttered roll filled with cheese and know exactly where we are on the map. It might be a doorstep of Granary eaten with a mature farmhouse Cheddar, tomato chutney, and pickled onions (the Great British tradition of Ploughman's), or Jarlsberg with a whole grain "grovbrød" if we travel north to Norway, or, if we happen to be lucky enough to be lazing in the shade of an olive grove in Tuscany, some of that long-lasting unsalted "filone" with a hunk of ewe's milk "Pecorino Toscano."

Wearing my practical hat, then, I should advise you to stick to hard cheeses: a mature **Gouda**, **cheddar**, or **Cantal** (its French counterpart); and **hard sheep or goat cheeses,** such as **Spanish Manchego**, but this is to forego the delight of living dangerously and unwrapping a badly behaved **Époisses**, a cheese that is probably best eaten outdoors. You can always bury the remains rather than lugging them back home again.

Pan out your finds with a relish, some unshelled nuts and big bunches of grapes, and some figs or whatever other fruit is in season. Any hearty bread is good, a sourdough or a whole grain, but there is no real need for butter, with a bunch of watercress, perhaps, or some other that pays lip service to green and leafy.

OVEN-BAKED SWEET TOMATO AND CHILE RELISH

Challenged to a competition to come up with the most ways of consuming a sweet tomato and chile relish, my family would eat any other for breakfast. Pared down to the bare minimum, this take on it is cooked in the oven, so there's no hovering over the stove. It will last in the fridge for many weeks, unless your last name is Bell.

Makes approx. 1⅔ to 2 cups
(1 to 2 jam jars)

2¼ pounds vine tomatoes
¾ teaspoon sea salt
1 cup granulated granulated sugar with
   pectin (see package instructions)
1 tablespoon finely chopped medium-hot
   red chile
3 garlic cloves, peeled and finely chopped
⅓ cup plus 1 tablespoon white wine or
   cider vinegar.

Preheat the oven to 400°F. Bring a large pot of water to a boil, cut out a cone from the top of each tomato to remove the core, and plunge them into the boiling water for about 20 seconds, and then into cold water. Slip off the skins and coarsely chop the tomato flesh. Combine all the ingredients in a large roasting pan (10 x 14 inches) and place in the oven, uncovered, for 65 to 75 minutes, giving the relish a stir toward the end. It should reduce considerably, with the tomatoes sitting in a small amount of syrupy juices. Spoon it into a hot sterilized jar, or jars, cover, and let cool. Store in the fridge.

EGG MAYONNAISE SALADINIS

Those on carb-free regimes can find picnics quite challenging, the role played by bread and tarts being the starring one that it is. So, these "saladinis" are a great stand-in, but if carbs aren't an issue, then buttered buns with egg mayonnaise are ever a joy.

On record we may have foresworn sliced white for whole grain, but this doesn't include mini hot dog buns. The shape of these make them a winner for passing around at picnics, and you could of course make them up as closed rolls and cut them in half, in which case you will need twice as many, but they are rather dainty in their open form.

Anchovies are particularly savory and fine here, but egg salad can be partnered with all manner of goodies—a thick wad of garden cress, air-dried ham or crispy snippets of bacon, sundried tomatoes or a teaspoon of salmon or trout roe if you want to up the ante. Or, if asked to bring a plate of something to a celebratory picnic, make up two or three of these, as well as some "saladinis."

Makes 6 to 8

5 medium eggs
4 tablespoons mayonnaise
sea salt and black pepper

approx. 3 Boston lettuce hearts, outer leaves
  discarded, or 3 to 4 mini hot dog buns
6 to 8 anchovy fillets, halved lengthwise
unsalted butter, softened for spreading (optional)

Bring a medium saucepan of water to a boil, lower in the eggs using a spoon, and boil for 10 minutes. Drain, refill the pan with cold water, and let the eggs cool. Now shell them and cut off and discard the ½ inch or so of white. In a bowl, mash the yolks with the mayonnaise and a bit of seasoning to a coarse paste, and finely chop and fold in the whites. You can make the egg salad up to 24 hours in advance, in which case cover and chill it.

For saladinis
Separate out the Boston lettuce hearts. You want leaves 2¾ inches long; reserve anything bigger or smaller for a salad. Fill with the egg salad and drape a strip of anchovy on top of each one.

For rolls
Slice a thin sliver off the top of the rolls and slit in half (you can also slice the bottom crust off if desired). Butter (if wished), spread with the egg salad, and drape a couple of anchovy strips on top of each one.

RETRO CLUBS

Little squared sandwiches are great when you want a big plate of something.

Makes approx. 25

approx. 8 slices honey-baked ham,
    fat removed
Dijon mustard
unsalted butter, softened for spreading
8 slices white bread (medium), crusts
    removed
½ cucumber, peeled and thinly sliced
approx. two thirds of a 7-ounce jar
    pimento-stuffed green olives

Line a 9-inch square baking pan (i.e. brownie pan) with plastic wrap, leaving enough overhanging the sides to fold back over the top. Arrange half the ham in a layer over the bottom and spread with a bit of mustard. Lightly butter the bread on either side and arrange a layer on top of the ham, cutting it to fit the pan. Lay the cucumber in a single layer on top in rows of overlapping slices, then top with more bread, spread with a bit of mustard, and finish with the ham. Fold the overhanging plastic wrap over the top and press the sandwich down with your hands.

Open the plastic wrap up, turn the sandwich onto a board, and peel off the plastic wrap that lined the bottom. Tidy the edges with a bread knife, then cut into about 25 small square sandwiches. Skewer each one with an olive, sticking the toothpick through the stack. Carefully remove to a serving plate with an offset spatula. These can be made well in advance, the night before if wished; chill and keep covered in plastic wrap to transport.

SMOKED SALMON AND CREAM CHEESE ROLLS

The best smoked salmon rolls and bagels come with a thick blanket of soft creamy cheese laced with chives, and peppered with cayenne. These are another good plate for sharing, either cut in half or in quarters. Mini-bagels are also an option, but ultimately any roll will do.

Makes 4

Cream cheese
²/₃ cup cream cheese
3 tablespoons fromage frais
a generous squeeze of lemon juice
a few drops of onion juice (squeezed
    through a garlic press)
2 tablespoons finely chopped chives
Rolls
unsalted butter, softened for spreading
    (optional)
4 rolls, slit
7 ounces sliced smoked salmon
cayenne pepper
watercress sprigs, to serve (optional)

In a bowl, beat the cream cheese with the fromage frais, then beat in the lemon and onion juice, and mix in the chives. Butter the rolls, if wished, and spread the cream cheese mix on the lower half, then top with smoked salmon, dust with cayenne, and arrange a few sprigs of watercress on top, if wished. Close and halve or quarter.

ANCHOVY BUNS

Made in a mini muffin pan, these are of a size that leaves plenty of space to sample everything else on offer. Lovely on their own, it's tempting to dish them up with sour cream and salmon roe too.

Makes 12

3 tablespoons unsalted butter, melted, plus extra for greasing the pan
1 cup plus 3 tablespoons all-purpose flour
1 heaping teaspoon baking powder, sifted
sea salt
cayenne pepper
2 medium eggs
½ cup plus 1 tablespoon milk
6 salted anchovy fillets, thinly sliced
6 scallions, trimmed and thinly sliced
1 teaspoon extra virgin olive oil

Preheat the oven to 400°F, and liberally grease a 12-cup mini muffin pan with butter. In a large bowl, combine the flour, baking powder, and a pinch of salt and cayenne pepper. In another large bowl, whisk the eggs and milk, then stir in the melted butter. Pour this mixture onto the dry ingredients and blend to a lumpy batter. Fold in the anchovies and three quarters of the scallions, then half-fill the cups with the mixture.

Toss the reserved scallion with the olive oil and scatter this over the top of the buns. Bake for 15 to 17 minutes, until golden and crusty. These can also be rewarmed for 5 to 10 minutes in an oven heated to 375°F to refresh them if they are a day or two old.

CHEESE AND ONION MUFFINS

A classic combination that never fails.

Makes 12

1¾ cups all-purpose flour
½ cup fine cornmeal
½ cup finely grated pecorino
1 tablespoon baking powder
½ teaspoon sea salt
3 medium eggs
¾ cup plus 3 tablespoons milk
1/3 cup unsalted butter, melted
1²/3 cups crumbled Caerphilly cheese
8 scallions, trimmed and thinly sliced
1 teaspoon finely chopped medium-hot red chile
1 teaspoon extra virgin olive oil

Preheat the oven to 425°F, and arrange 12 paper muffin liners inside a muffin pan. In a large bowl, combine the flour, cornmeal, grated pecorino, baking powder, and salt. In another large bowl, beat the eggs and milk, then stir in the melted butter. Pour this mixture onto the dry ingredients and beat to a lumpy batter. Fold in 1 heaping cup of the Caerphilly, three quarters of the scallions, and the chile and fill the paper liners to within ½ inch of the top.

Toss the reserved scallion with the olive oil and scatter this over the top of the muffins, then scatter over the rest of the Caerphilly. Bake for 10 minutes, then turn the oven down to 375°F and bake for another 15 minutes. Serve them warm or newly cooled.

SCOTCH EGG PIE

This halfway house between a pork pie and a Scotch egg avoids the difficult parts involved in both.

For 6 to 8 people/Makes one 8½-inch terrine

Crust
3⅔ cups plus 2 tablespoons all-purpose flour
½ cup plus 1 tablespoon unsalted butter, chilled
   and diced, plus extra for greasing the pan
½ cup plus 1 tablespoon shortening, chilled
   and diced
1 medium egg yolk
milk or water

Filling
6 medium eggs
1¾ pounds meaty pork sausage, e.g. Toulouse
1 tablespoon finely chopped rosemary
1 tablespoon finely chopped sage
1 banana or 2 round shallots, peeled and finely
   chopped
sea salt and black pepper
1 tablespoon Dijon mustard
1 egg yolk beaten with 1 tablespoon milk (eggwash)

Make the pie crust: In a food processor, give the flour, butter, and shortening a quick burst at high speed to reduce it to a crumb-like consistency. Add the egg yolk and enough milk or water to bring the dough together, wrap it in plastic wrap, and chill for 1 hour or overnight. In the meantime, bring a medium saucepan of water to a boil and simmer the eggs for 7 minutes. Drain, refill with cold, and let cool.

Preheat the oven to 375°F. Grease and line the bottom and long sides of a 8½-inch (5½-cup) loaf pan with parchment paper, leaving it overhanging the sides. Cut a long strip to line the bottom and ends, again so that it overhangs. Slit the sausage casings and slip the meat into a large bowl, then add the herbs, the shallots, and some seasoning and work with your hands or a spoon until evenly blended. Shell the eggs and cut off the ends of white to just reveal the yolk.

Roll out two thirds of the pie dough to 1/8 to ¼ inch thick on a lightly floured work surface into a rectangular shape large enough to line the bottom and sides of the pan, with some overhanging, and lay it in place. Trim any excess, leaving a ¾-inch leeway, and roll these out with the remaining third of the dough large enough to form a lid. Press about a third of the sausage meat into the pan, then make a shallow trough down the center and lay the eggs with each yolk touching the next in a line along the center. Fill with the remaining sausage meat, pressing it well down. Brush the mustard over the top of the sausage meat, brush the pastry edges with eggwash, and lay the rolled sheet of pastry on top, pressing the edges together well to seal the pie, then trim level with the pan. Brush the surface with the eggwash, make a few slits in the top, and bake for 1½ hours.

Remove and let cool for 30 minutes. Carefully loosen the pie by lifting it a short way out of the pan using the paper overhang, then let it settle back again. Let cool completely and then chill, preferably overnight, before carefully lifting out and gently peeling off the paper—I would recommend transporting it in its pan, paper and all, though you could also cut and lay it out on a large serving plate.

Kit Serrated knife, plate

SIMPLE SPANISH TORTILLA

I don't think you can beat the austerity of a classic potato and onion tortilla. A humble basic but so delicious, you don't even have to run to the Parmesan and herbs if you want something truly plain; it will still prove to take the starring role.

For 4 to 6 people

extra virgin olive oil
18 ounces medium new or red potatoes, peeled
  or scrubbed as necessary and thickly sliced
sea salt and black pepper

⅓ cup plus 1 tablespoon water
2 onions, peeled, halved, and finely sliced
6 medium eggs
¼ cup finely sliced Parmesan (optional)
2 tablespoons marjoram leaves (optional)

In a 9½-inch nonstick skillet with a heatproof handle, heat 2 tablespoons of extra virgin olive oil over medium heat, add the potatoes, and cook them until they are coated in the oil, about 5 minutes, turning them now and again. Season them with salt and add the water to the pan, then cover it with a large saucepan lid and cook over low heat until the potatoes are just tender, about 10 minutes. Using the lid, drain off any excess water and carefully transfer the potatoes to a large bowl.

Wipe the pan out with paper towels, then return it to medium heat, add another couple of tablespoons of olive oil, and sauté the onions until golden, 7 to 10 minutes, stirring frequently and seasoning them at the end. Mix them into the potatoes.

To cook the omelet, beat the eggs in a bowl with a bit of seasoning, then pour them onto the potatoes and onions and gently stir to combine. Preheat the broiler to high, and pop the skillet in which you cooked the vegetables over medium heat. Add a tablespoon of olive oil to the pan, add the egg and potato mixture, level the surface, and cook for 3 minutes. Scatter the Parmesan slices over the top of the omelet, and then the marjoram leaves, if including. Drizzle over another tablespoon of oil and place under the broiler until golden and sizzling, 3 minutes. It should still be slightly moist in the center but will firm up as it cools.

Kit Sharp knife, plate

ASPARAGUS AND
SMOKED SALMON FRITTATA

This is a lively take on an omelet; the lemon, chile, and parsley together give the traditional duo of asparagus and smoked salmon a bit of warm weather appeal.

For 4 people

7 ounces finger-thick asparagus, trimmed weight
6 medium eggs
½ teaspoon finely grated lemon zest, plus
   1 tablespoon lemon juice

2 teaspoons finely chopped medium-hot
   red chile
4 tablespoons coarsely chopped flat-leaf parsley
3½ ounces sliced smoked salmon, brown meat
   cut off, and cut into strips 1¼- to 1½-inch wide
2 tablespoons extra virgin olive oil

Bring a large pot of salted water to a boil and simmer the asparagus spears until just tender, 4 to 5 minutes. Drain them in a colander and pass them under cold running water to stop them cooking any more.

In a large bowl, beat the eggs, then beat in the lemon zest and juice, the chile, and 3 tablespoons of parsley. Gently mix in the salmon and the asparagus spears.

Preheat the broiler to high, and also place a 9½-inch skillet with a heatproof handle over medium heat. Heat a tablespoon of oil in the pan, add the frittata mixture, leveling the asparagus, and cook for 3 minutes. Scatter the remaining parsley over the top of the omelet, drizzle over another tablespoon of oil, and place under the broiler until golden and puffy at the sides, 3 to 4 minutes.

Kit Sharp knife, plate

PASTA TIMBALE WITH LEEKS AND GOAT CHEESE

A great veggie main that makes a change from a savory tart or omelet. This is good made with those giant pastas that look as though they might dwarf any sauce you put their way; tubular ones especially provide a welcome structure for the pie.

For 6 people

9 ounces dry tortiglioni
extra virgin olive oil
3 leeks, trimmed and sliced
sea salt and black pepper
3 garlic cloves, peeled and finely chopped
2 tablespoons lemon thyme leaves

1 cup freshly grated Parmesan
3 medium eggs, plus 1 egg yolk
1¼ cups heavy cream
⅔ cup milk
7 ounces medium-sharp goat cheese (weight excluding rind), cut into ½-inch dice
6 tablespoons coarsely chopped flat-leaf parsley

Preheat the oven to 400°F. Bring a large pot of salted water to a boil, add the tortiglioni, give it a stir, and cook for about two thirds of the recommended time, then drain into a colander, return to the pan, and toss with a dash of olive oil.

At the same time, in a large skillet, heat a couple of tablespoons of oil over medium heat, add the leeks, season, and sauté until they have started to soften and are lightly colored, 5 to 7 minutes, adding the garlic and half the thyme just before the end.

Brush a tablespoon of oil over the bottom of an 8-inch cake pan 2¾ inches deep, with a tightly fitting but removable collar, and scatter over a couple of tablespoons of the Parmesan. In a large bowl, beat together the eggs and yolk, cream, milk, and seasoning. Reserving a couple of tablespoons of the Parmesan, mix in the remainder. Fold in the leeks, pasta, two thirds of the goat cheese, and the parsley.

Place the pan on a cookie sheet, fill with the mixture, and press down with your hands so that the ingredients are level and as far as possible submerged. Scatter over the remaining Parmesan, goat cheese, and thyme. Drizzle over another tablespoon of oil and bake for 45 to 50 minutes, until set and golden, and there is no evidence of liquid in the center if you pierce it with a knife.

Let cool. It is at its best eaten freshly cool, but can also be covered and chilled, in which case bring it back up to room temperature before serving.

Kit Sharp knife, plate, knife and fork

PEA TART "À LA FRANÇAISE"

Of all the alternatives to a Quiche Lorraine, I find that a pea tart is the one that seems to go down best, not least because children love it. Do cheat and buy ready-made pie dough if time is tight, but ideally all-butter.

For 6 people

Crust
1¾ cups all-purpose flour
a pinch of sea salt
⅔ cup unsalted butter, chilled and diced
1 medium egg, separated
cold water
Filling
2 tablespoons unsalted butter
½ teaspoon sugar

sea salt and black pepper
2¾ cups fresh green peas
2 bunches scallions (approx. 4½ ounces each),
   trimmed and sliced
1 Boston lettuce heart, thinly sliced
1¼ cups heavy cream
2 medium eggs, plus 1 yolk
a handful of mint leaves, torn (optional)
1½ cups freshly grated Parmesan

Place the flour and salt in the bowl of a food processor, add the butter, and reduce to a fine crumb-like consistency. Incorporate the egg yolk and then, with the motor running, trickle in just enough cold water for the dough to cling together in lumps. Wrap the dough in plastic wrap and chill for at least 1 hour.

Preheat the oven to 400°F. Knead the dough until it is pliable. Thinly roll it out on a lightly floured work surface and carefully lift it into a 9-inch tart/quiche pan 2½ inches deep with a removable bottom, pressing it into the corner of the pan and running a rolling pin over the top to trim the edge. Reserve the trimmings. Prick the bottom with a fork and line it with a sheet of foil, tucking it over the top to secure the dough side to the pan. Now weight it down with dried beans.

Bake the pastry shell for 15 minutes, then remove the foil and beans. If any of the side has shrunk more than it should, use a bit of the reserved dough to patch them. Brush the bottom and side of the shell with the reserved egg white, then bake it for another 10 minutes, until it is lightly colored.

In the meantime, make the filling: In a large saucepan, place ⅔ cup water with the butter, sugar, and ½ teaspoon of salt. Bring to a boil over high heat, add the peas, and cook until tender, 5 minutes, stirring occasionally. Drain them into a strainer.

Reserving a couple of tablespoons of the scallions, place the remainder in a small saucepan with the lettuce, the cream, and some seasoning. Bring to a boil, then cover with a lid, leaving a gap for the steam to escape, and simmer for 5 minutes. In a large bowl, beat the eggs and yolk, then beat in the cream and onion mixture and fold in the peas, the mint, if including, and half the Parmesan. Transfer the filling to the tart shell and scatter over the remaining Parmesan and scallions. Bake the tart on a preheated cookie sheet for 35 to 40 minutes, until golden and set in the center. Transport in the pan.

Kit Sharp knife, plate

CHERRY TOMATO AND PARMESAN GALETTES

Pizza-like in their appeal, children are unlikely to notice the crust is that little bit more delicate. These are just the right size for one per person, but cut up are also good as a communal offering to pass around.

For 6 people

10½ ounces puff pastry
Dijon mustard
2 cups cherry tomatoes, halved

1 medium egg yolk beaten with 1 tablespoon water (eggwash)
sea salt and black pepper
¼ heaping cup finely shaved Parmesan
extra virgin olive oil

Preheat the oven to 425°F. Thinly roll out the pastry on a lightly floured work surface—you can do this half at a time if it's easier—and cut out six 4½-inch circles using a bowl or plate as a guide. Arrange these on a couple of cookie sheets.

Spread a bit of Dijon mustard in the center of each circle, to within about ¾ inch of the rim. Place the tomatoes on top. Brush the surrounding rim with the eggwash, then season the tomatoes, cover with a few slivers of Parmesan, and drizzle over some olive oil. Bake in the oven for 15 to 20 minutes, until golden and risen.

SALADS

Some years ago my husband and I

were on a trip to California, to visit the wonderful varietal garden attached to the Fetzer vineyards in Hopland, Mendocino County, to the north of San Francisco. Being rather green to the culture of Highway 101, we arrived there late afternoon devoid of any provisions. We were staying within the grounds of the garden, but hadn't realized there was nothing for miles around save a small general store close to the gates that didn't stock much more than popcorn and canned tuna, and it had closed in any case. So we found ourselves, shut into the garden of paradise as the sun went down, with row upon row of wonderful ripe heirloom tomatoes, a fridge of delicious Fetzer wines to choose from, and a pot of salt and some oil in the pantry, and that was it. By the time we went to bed I felt like Peter Rabbit locked into Mr. McGregor's garden overnight, drunk on carrot juice, or a wasp trapped in a jam factory. But it was one of the most memorable feasts I can recall.

A couple of beautiful, ripe beefsteak tomatoes is still my idea of plenty on a picnic. Or I might take some tightly closed heads of Belgian endive, or Boston hearts, by way of something green and leafy for dipping into the juices turning to jelly below the roast chicken in its foil. And if I do want to ratchet it up, then the classics of potato salad and coleslaw are classics for a reason—they jostle with all those cold cuts, pies, and the like with just the right kind of informality.

Though one other ruse, for when you want to take either an all-in-one or something that little bit more sophisticated, is the layered salad. Here by arranging the dressing and slightly heavier ingredients in the bottom of the dish, and working up to the leafier and more delicate ones, you can assemble everything you might want on your picnic in a single bowl, and simply toss it before eating. Perfect for that snatched interval at an outdoor opera or school sports day.

"A couple of beautiful, ripe beefsteak tomatoes is my idea of plenty on a picnic."

LET'S GO: CRUDITÉS

Raw slivers of vegetables often fare better than delicate salad greens. Middle Eastern restaurants make a virtue out of the simplicity of crudités, flatbreads, and a small saucer of oil for dipping and another of sea salt, while the Italians refer to the dipping of raw vegetables into olive oil and then salt as "pinzimonio."

For a picnic, crudités do away with the need for a salad, so they're a great last-minute solution that you can add to with dips, cheeses, pâté, and cold meats. A few carefully chosen and prepared vegetables add an essential homemade touch.

Trim and wash crudités before leaving and transport in an airtight container, in water with ice cubes for maximum freshness if there is likely to be any substantial length of time before you eat them. You can take some unbreakable beverage cups to arrange them in, or lightweight bowls. Also, take parsley, olive oil, an envelope of sea salt—you can twist this up in a piece of parchment paper, and some bread.

TOMATOES

A couple of big, misshapen beefsteak tomatoes and an envelope of sea salt provide one of the great rustic solutions on a picnic. Hack them into wedges for eating with a cold roast chicken, or slices of honey-baked ham and runny cheeses.

Otherwise, a carton of cherry tomatoes can be the starting point for a selection of crudités. If it's just two of you, then look for a mixed carton. For any number of people, cartons of different cherry or other tomato varieties will make a big splash— baby plum tomatoes, cocktail cherry ones, red, yellow, and orange, on the vine and off.

RADISHES

Long breakfast radishes are especially good. Give the bunch a good wash under cold running water before leaving home and simply trim them once you get there.

RED AND YELLOW BELL PEPPERS

Strips of bell pepper make for sweet and tender eating. Cut these as close to the time of eating as possible so that they are crisp and fresh.

CELERY HEARTS

The heart of any head of celery has the most pronounced flavor and promises to be tender too. The stalk's naturally curved shape can support all manner of dips.

SCALLIONS

The slim ones are best for munching with cheese and cold meats, so trim them just before leaving home.

BABY CARROTS

Trim the stalk ends and peel if necessary, depending on their size.

A CRISP GREEN SALAD

With a bit of strategic thinking, some of the simplest salads are also the best and can be assembled once you arrive at your destination. Be selective about the greens with the right frills or extras and a two-ingredient dressing whisked up before you go, and you'll have a salad that will far outstrip any packaged offering.

CHOOSING SALAD LEAVES

The original bags of **mixed salad greens**, pioneered by the French cooperative Florette, are still a fine convenience. The downside to this genre are many of the copycat bags that include parts of the leaf that we would rather not be eating, or they are tired, whereby the convenience turns into the inconvenience of having to sort through them and rid them of any browning parts.

Single leaves tend to fare better than mixed (at least they wilt at the same rate), so you can tell by looking at them whether or not they are fresh. A bag of **watercress**, **arugula**, or a carton of **garden cress** are all good choices. Beyond this, young tightly closed heads of lettuce such as **Boston and Romaine hearts**, and heads of **Belgian endive** need only have the base sliced off and the outer leaves discarded, before separating out the crisp and tender leaves within. I love munching on **flat-leaf parsley** in the company of salty cold cuts, or with a sliver of cheese and chutney—it provides a breath of fresh air, clean and sweet.

Floppy round lettuces can also be put to good use. Discard any leathery outer leaves, and give the lettuce a good rinse under cold running water, then shake dry. Twist off the base and place whole in a cupped bowl, then loosen the leaves as though you were opening out a flower and scatter over some **snipped chives**. Drizzle over a **vinaigrette** to serve.
Allow one for 2 to 4 people

SALAD DRESSINGS

When it comes to salad dressings, there's no need to run to more than two ingredients, or four if you count the salt and pepper. Whisk it before leaving and have it ready in a small clip-top storage container or empty jam jar.

Vinaigrette dressing

Shake a tablespoon of **balsamic vinegar or lemon juice** with some **sea salt** and ground **black pepper** in a small clip-top container or jar. Add 3 tablespoons of **extra virgin olive oil** and shake again. Or, for something slightly more exotic, you could extend this to a t**omato, passion fruit, or fig vinegar**, for instance, and a **walnut or hazelnut oil**.
For 6 people

Creamy Mustard Dressing

Beat 2/3 cup **sour cream** with 2 heaping teaspoons of **Dijon mustard**, a generous pinch of **sugar**, and a bit of **sea salt** and chill.
For 6 people

Cheat's Mayonnaise

Beat 3 tablespoons of **mayonnaise** and 3 tablespoons of **sour cream** with a bit of sugar, and **sea salt**.
For 6 people

SALAD EXTRAS

● Pine nuts, toasted or untoasted ● Pumpkin seeds ● Macadamia nuts ● Roasted salted cashews ● Roasted salted almonds ● Green or black olives, marinated or stuffed ● Herb leaves—mint, flat-leaf parsley, dill ● Cherry tomatoes ● Diced feta ● Parmesan shavings

PICNIC COLESLAW

I only have to see pictures of 4th of July picnics and the Stars and Stripes to think "coleslaw." And why not? It's easy to see why a big, creamy bowl of the stuff is a staple—it travels like a pro and all that dressing is great with cold roast chicken, sausage, and the like. Refinement in a coleslaw rests with slicing that head of cabbage wafer fine, so sharpen up the knives.

For 6 people

½ cup Greek-style yogurt
4 tablespoons mayonnaise
½ tablespoon white wine or tarragon vinegar
½ tablespoon superfine sugar
sea salt
½ small head of savoy cabbage
2 slim carrots, peeled and finely diagonally sliced
3 slim scallions, trimmed and finely sliced
2 stalks of celery heart, finely sliced
½ cup chopped walnuts (optional)

In a large bowl, beat together the yogurt, mayonnaise, vinegar, sugar, and a bit of salt. Quarter the cabbage, cut out the core, and slice wafer thin, then halve the strands. Reserving a bit of the carrot and a third of the scallion, toss the remainder into the dressing along with the cabbage, celery, and walnuts, if including. Spoon into a transportable container or serving bowl and then scatter over the reserved carrot and scallion.

Kit Serving spoon, plate, fork

NEW POTATO, ROASTED RED ONION, AND CASHEW SALAD

This is one step up in sophistication from the potato salad on page 86, more in line with the boutique patisserie fare we have come to love. It's worth taking any leftover salad back home with you, as it can be sliced and sautéed or made into a tortilla a day or so later.

For 6 people

2¾ pounds small new potatoes, unpeeled, scrubbed if necessary
6 tablespoons extra virgin olive oil
2 tablespoons dry vermouth or white wine
sea salt and black pepper

4 red onions, peeled, halved, and thinly sliced
2 tablespoons tarragon leaves
3 tablespoons snipped chives
¾ cup roasted cashews

Preheat the oven to 400°F. Meanwhile, bring a large pot of salted water to a boil. Halve any large potatoes so they are all roughly the same size, add to the pan, and boil until tender, 20 to 25 minutes. Drain them in a strainer and let stand for a few minutes for the surface moisture to evaporate. Transfer them to a large bowl and toss with 4 tablespoons of the olive oil, the vermouth or wine, and some seasoning, and let cool.

At the same time as the potatoes are cooking, toss the onions in a bowl with the remaining 2 tablespoons of oil and spread them out in a thin layer on a couple of cookie sheets. Roast for 20 to 25 minutes, until golden, giving them a stir halfway through to ensure they color evenly. Let cool.

Toss the roasted onion, herbs, and nuts into the potatoes before leaving.

Kit Serving spoon, plate, fork

DELI COUNTER POTATO SALAD

A great basic. Here, a bit of sour cream mixed with some jarred mayo softens the edges, and fresh parsley works wonders to bring it to life. Yummy with roast chicken, tail-on cooked shrimp, and lightly boiled eggs (hens' eggs 7 to 8 minutes or quail eggs 2½ minutes).

For 4 people

26 ounces small new potatoes, peeled
  or scrubbed
Dressing
⅓ cup plus 1 tablespoon sour cream
⅓ cup plus 1 tablespoon mayonnaise
sea salt
1 tablespoon finely chopped shallot

2 tablespoons small capers (such as
  nonpareille), rinsed
2 tablespoons finely chopped flat-leaf parsley,
  plus extra to serve
cayenne pepper (optional)

Bring a large pot of salted water to a boil, add the potatoes, and cook until tender, then drain in a colander. Let cool and then dice.

In a bowl, beat together the sour cream and mayonnaise with a pinch of salt. Stir in the shallot, capers, and parsley, and then the potatoes. Transfer to a transportable bowl or container. Dust with cayenne pepper, if wished, and scatter over some more parsley.

Kit Serving spoon, plate, fork

QUINOA TABBOULEH

Quinoa makes for an almost better picnic tabbouleh than bulgur wheat. Lusciously soft and comforting, this salad can stand in for potato or pasta while being every bit as vibrant and lively as the Middle Eastern classic. You'll need nice big bunches of herbs for this, just the tender young leaves. And as ever you want really good tomatoes; they don't have to be cherry—any type that promise to be sweet and juicy will do the trick. You could also stir some diced feta into the salad at the very end, about 1½ cups of ¾-inch dice.

For 4 to 6 people

1¼ scant cups dry quinoa
3 tablespoons lemon juice
2 tablespoons water
sea salt and black pepper
8 tablespoons extra virgin olive oil
⅓ cup coarsely chopped young mint
  leaves

2¾ ounces young flat-leaf parsley leaves,
  coarsely chopped
1⅔ cups cherry tomatoes, halved or quartered
  depending on their size
6 scallions, trimmed and thinly sliced

Bring a medium saucepan of salted water to a boil. Heat a large skillet over medium heat, scatter the quinoa over the bottom, and toast for a few minutes, stirring frequently, until it gives off a lovely warming aroma and starts popping. Transfer to a bowl and let cool for a few minutes, then add to the boiling water and simmer until tender, 15 to 20 minutes. Drain through a strainer, return it to the pan, cover, and let cool.

In a small airtight container, whisk the lemon juice with the water and some seasoning, then whisk in the oil. In a large bowl or container, combine the herbs, tomatoes, scallions, and quinoa. You can prepare the salad to this point up to a couple of hours in advance, in which case cover and take the dressing separately, and pour this over and mix at the time.

Kit Serving spoon, plate, fork

PESTO MACARONI SALAD

A layered salad with a zesty pesto dressing and cherry tomatoes that also doubles as a hot pasta dish with a minute or two's warming in a saucepan over a gas flame if you are in need of something warming on a picnic (see pages 120 to 143). Essentially it takes no time at all to prepare, but it is worth investing in a decent jar of pesto. (For 4 to 6 people, scale it down to 7 ounces pasta, ¾ pound tomatoes, 5 tablespoons of olive oil, and 2 of pesto, respectively.)

For 6 to 8 people

10½ ounces dry macaroni or penne
7 tablespoons extra virgin olive oil
sea salt and black pepper
14 ounces to 1 pound baby plum or
    mixed cherry tomatoes, halved
3 tablespoons pesto
a couple of handfuls of coarsely chopped
    flat-leaf parsley

Bring a large pot of salted water to a boil, add the pasta, give it a stir, and cook until just tender. Drain in a colander, briefly place under cold running water to stop any more cooking, then toss with a tablespoon of the olive oil in a bowl and let cool. At the same time, in another bowl, season the tomatoes with salt and let stand for 15 to 30 minutes.

In a large serving bowl, whisk the pesto, remaining oil, and a bit of seasoning. Scatter the tomatoes on top, drizzling over any juices given out, then scatter over the pasta and, finally, the parsley. Toss to serve when you're ready to eat.

Kit Serving spoon, plate, fork

PEA AND MINT SALAD

These veggies will happily sit for days in the fridge, drinking up the garlic and mint, as long as you season them with lemon at the last minute.

For 4 to 6 people

2½ cups fresh green peas
2 cups stem-end-trimmed snow peas
2 cups trimmed sugar snap peas
2 to 3 garlic cloves, peeled and crushed to a paste
2 shallots, peeled and finely chopped
4 strips of lemon zest
9 tablespoons extra virgin olive oil
a couple of large handfuls of mint leaves, coarsely chopped
1 tablespoon sesame seeds
sea salt and black pepper
a couple of squeezes of lemon juice

Bring a large pot of salted water to a boil. Add the green peas and cook for 3 minutes, adding the snow peas and sugar peas after 2 minutes. Drain into a colander and refresh them under cold running water, then let stand for a few minutes for the surface moisture to evaporate.

In a large bowl, combine the garlic, shallot, lemon zest, and olive oil, add the cooked peas, and toss to coat them. Let cool, then mix in the mint and sesame seeds. Cover and chill overnight, or longer if you want, although you can eat the salad immediately, too.

Discard the lemon zest and season with salt and pepper before leaving home, and take a lemon with you to squeeze over just before serving.

Kit Serving spoon, plate, fork

CHERRY TOMATO SALAD

A simple tomato salad, like a potato salad, is a wonderful picnic basic. This lively rendition lends itself in particular to the Middle Eastern palate, so think hummus and olives, pickled chiles, and salty sheep cheeses. On the same note, you can make a salad of sliced **tomatoes** with a drizzle of **extra virgin olive oil**, a sprinkling of **sea salt,** and a fine dusting of **ground sumac**, the sharp-tasting rust-red berries. Or sprinkle over **za'atar**, a blend of ground sesame seeds, dried thyme, sumac, and sea salt. Failing this, **dried oregano or mint** is ever a delicious touch.

For 4 people

4 cups mixed cherry tomatoes, halved or quartered, depending on size
sugar
sea salt
4 tablespoons extra virgin olive oil
2 tablespoons lemon juice
1 large shallot, peeled, halved, and finely chopped
4 tablespoons coarsely chopped flat-leaf parsley

In a bowl or other container, toss the tomatoes with a bit of sugar and salt. Let stand for 15 to 30 minutes. Pour over the olive oil and lemon juice, then scatter over the shallot and parsley and gently toss.

Kit Serving spoon, plate, fork

CUCUMBER, CHILE, AND PUMPKIN SEED SALAD

This has a clean, gazpacho-like charm, laced with chile, scallions, and lemon, it would be lovely with Gravlax (see page 45), Poolside Shrimp (see page 140), or the Grand Salmon (see page 119). There is no need to peel the cucumbers here; the salt works its magic on the skin, which ends up as tender as the inside with just a slight crunch.

For 6 to 8 people

2 cucumbers, ends discarded, halved,
   seeded, and sliced into half-moons
   about ⅛ inch thick
sea salt
⅓ heaping cup pumpkin seeds or pine nuts
4 tablespoons extra virgin olive oil
2 tablespoons lemon juice
3 scallions, trimmed and finely sliced
½ medium-hot red chile, seeded and
   finely chopped
a handful of coarsely chopped cilantro

In a large bowl, season the cucumber with sea salt and let stand for 30 minutes. Give the cucumber a good rinse in a strainer or a sink of cold water, then dry it in batches between double thicknesses of paper towels. At the same time, heat a skillet over medium heat and toast the pumpkin seeds or pine nuts until lightly colored, stirring continuously, then transfer them to a bowl and let cool.

In a serving bowl or sealable container, combine the oil and lemon juice. Scatter the cucumber on top of the salad, then the scallion, chile, cilantro, and seeds or nuts, and cover to transport. Toss the salad in the dressing just before serving.

Kit Serving spoon, plate, fork

CHARBROILED BROCCOLI AND SESAME SALAD

Long-stemmed baby broccoli has replaced asparagus in my affections, and charbroiling renders it sweet but with a delicious faint bitterness. These spears are great finger food but also make a good basic that can be dressed up. Beyond sesame seeds, which are an instant finishing touch, maybe turn it into a salad with strips of Medjool dates and ripe tomatoes, or add some cooked fava beans, pine nuts, and the like. You can forego the sesame seeds, if you prefer, and simply charbroil the broccoli with olive oil.

For 4 people

14 ounces baby broccoli, trimmed
1 tablespoon sesame seeds
2 tablespoons peanut or vegetable oil

2 teaspoons sesame oil
sea salt and black pepper

Bring a large pot of salted water to a boil, add the broccoli, and cook for 3 minutes, then drain in a colander and let stand for a few minutes for the surface moisture to evaporate. In a small skillet, toast the sesame seeds over medium heat until lightly colored, stirring continuously, then transfer to a bowl and let cool.

Heat a ridged grill pan over medium heat. Beat together the peanut and sesame oils, pour over the broccoli, and toss, then season. Charbroil in two to three batches until golden or charred, 2 to 3 minutes each side, arranging the cooked spears on a plate or in a container as you go. Scatter over the sesame seeds.

Kit Serving spoon, plate

OVEN-ROAST RATATOUILLE

I turn to this again and again during the summer as my default way of cooking ratatouille. Not only do the vegetables concentrate in flavor in the oven but there is also no hovering over a hot pan, the last thing you want in serious heat. As ever this is a building block—it goes beautifully with fine shavings of Tomme de Savoie cheese, olives, and cured meats. And it's good for making the night before.

For 6 people

2¼ pounds beefsteak tomatoes, halved
   through the core
approx. 18 ounces eggplant, stem ends
   trimmed, halved lengthwise (or quartered if
   large), and thickly sliced
extra virgin olive oil
4 red bell peppers, cores and seeds removed
   and thinly sliced lengthwise
approx. 18 ounces zucchini, ends trimmed,
   halved lengthwise if large, and thickly sliced
sea salt and black pepper
3 red onions, peeled, halved, and sliced
4 garlic cloves, peeled and thinly sliced
a handful of coarsely chopped curly or
   flat-leaf parsley

Preheat the oven to 425°F. You will need three good-size roasting pans that will fit in the oven together. Arrange the tomatoes cut-side up in a tightly fitting single layer in one. Brush the eggplant with oil on both sides and arrange with the bell peppers and zucchini in another couple of roasting pans in a crowded layer—they will shrink as they cook. Drizzle a couple of tablespoons of olive oil over the tomatoes, and about 6 tablespoons over the other vegetables, and season everything.

Roast all three pans for 1 to 1¼ hours, stirring the onions and garlic into the peppers and zucchini after 30 minutes. Gently stir or turn them again 15 minutes later, concealing any well-colored vegetables below the surface, and continue to roast until well colored. Let all the vegetables cool.

Remove the skin from the tomatoes and cut out the hard core, then coarsely chop using a knife and fork. In a sealable bowl or container, combine all the vegetables, including the chopped tomatoes, to transport, gently folding in the parsley just before serving.

Kit Serving spoon, plate, fork

SLOW-ROAST TOMATOES

Just occasionally, and delightfully, work lands me on an elegant picnic somewhere exotic. One such occasion was in the South of France, outside St. Tropez in the shade of a vine, where lunch took the form of a beautiful selection of goat cheeses from the local market, a big arugula salad dressed with extra virgin olive oil and lemon juice, a large Le Parfait jar of slowly roasted tomatoes, and some sourdough bread. All told there was very little preparation involved, save the tomatoes that can be made well in advance, on a quiet midweek evening with the weekend in mind.

I've played with slow-roasting tomatoes endlessly over the years, and settled on this as the best method. There is no skinning or complicated preparation, just small sweet tomatoes rendered even sweeter after a couple of hours in a slow oven. But it's difficult to be too exact with timings—it will depend on the size of the tomatoes, how juicy they are, and how many you are cooking—so keep a watchful eye.

For 6 people/makes approx. 10½ ounces

4 cups cherry or cocktail tomatoes on the vine,
    halved
4 garlic cloves, skin-on and crushed
5 thyme sprigs
sea salt
sugar
extra virgin olive oil

Preheat the oven to 275°F. Lay the tomato halves skin-downwards in a single layer in a roasting pan lined with parchment paper. Scatter over the garlic and the thyme, pulling off half the leaves, and season with salt and a sprinkling of sugar. Drizzle over 3 tablespoons of olive oil and bake them until they are semi-dry and concentrated in flavor, but retaining some succulence, 1¾ to 2½ hours; they will reduce by about half their weight. Let cool.

If not serving straightaway, place them in a bowl or a jar and cover with olive oil. Chill for up to three days, bringing back up to room temperature before serving.

Kit Serving spoon, plate

ROASTED RED BELL PEPPER AND LENTIL SALAD

I used to cook this endlessly in the 1980s. Lentils and roasted peppers make a charmed marriage, especially good with goat cheese, olives, and salami. Should you want to take some roasted peppers on their own, then simply omit the lentils. This good-natured salad can be made several hours in advance and it will play happily to a mixed crowd of carnivores and vegetarians.

For 6 people

6 red bell peppers, cores and seeds removed,
   and quartered lengthwise
10 to 12 thyme sprigs
2 bay leaves
7 tablespoons extra virgin olive oil
sea salt and black pepper

1 head of garlic, cloves peeled
1 tablespoon balsamic vinegar
¾ cup dry French lentils (such as Le Puy)
coarsely chopped flat-leaf parsley, to serve
   (optional)

Preheat the oven to 425°F. Arrange the peppers in a crowded single layer in a large roasting pan and tuck the herbs between them. Drizzle over 4 tablespoons of the olive oil and season with salt and pepper. Roast for 25 minutes, then scatter over the garlic cloves, baste everything, and roast for another 15 to 25 minutes, or until golden and nicely singed. When the vegetables come out of the oven, drizzle over the vinegar and let cool.

At the same time, bring a medium saucepan of water to a boil and cook the lentils until tender but retaining their shape, 15 to 25 minutes. Drain into a strainer, briefly place under cold running water, and let cool.

Scatter the lentils over the peppers (discarding the thyme and bay), drizzle over the remaining oil, season with a bit more salt, and gently toss. Scatter with parsley, if wished, and cover to transport.

Kit Salad servers, plate, knife and fork

LAYERED NIÇOISE

I tend to return from France to London loaded with basics that I can't readily find once I am back. The checkout attendants at the local supermarket look at me curiously as they scan the twentieth bottle of Le Petit Marseillais shampoo, and the umpteenth can of fish. There is a huge differential between indifferent and very good sardines in oil, and tuna in water, and these are one of the basics of my pantry. Not that canned fish cannot be found in most major cities throughout the world, simply that Northern France and Spain make a delicacy out of this humble staple. The ideal for this salad is a good meaty whole chunk of fish that can be broken into neat chunks or coarsely flaked, rather than something that is on its way to being a pâté before you have even spooned it out of the can.

For 4 people

4 medium eggs
6 tablespoons extra virgin olive oil
1½ tablespoons lemon juice
sea salt and black pepper
2 tablespoons small capers, rinsed
2 (6- to 7-ounce) jars or cans of tuna in oil or
    spring water, drained

4 salted anchovy fillets, halved lengthwise
3 ripe plum or specialty tomatoes such as
    heirloom, cores cut out and cut into wedges
½ cup pitted green or black olives
2½–3 ounces arugula leaves

Bring a medium saucepan of water to a boil, add the eggs, and boil for 7 to 8 minutes to leave them slightly moist in the center. Drain and cool in cold water, then shell them and halve.

In a large deep salad bowl with room to spare for tossing once you have layered all the ingredients, whisk together the olive oil, lemon juice, some seasoning, and the capers. Dry the tuna on a double thickness of paper towels and break into chunks or coarsely flake. Add to the dressing and turn to coat everything. Lay the anchovy fillets on top, then the tomatoes and scatter over the olives. Finally, pile the aurugla on top and lay over the eggs.

Cover to transport and toss to serve once you are at the picnic.

Kit Serving spoon, plate, fork

COUSCOUS SALAD WITH PISTACHIOS AND POMEGRANATE

A couscous salad has become almost de rigueur on the picnic table. So much so that when a friend invited us to the opera at Glyndebourne this summer, with a "bring a salad" tagged on, this seemed the obvious choice. The only snag being that he had made one too, so it was a "couscous cook-off" as he put it, or something like turning up in the same dress. So, if you are going to provide a couscous salad, better make sure it's good, just in case.

For 6 people

1 cup vegetable stock
sea salt
a pinch of saffron threads (approx. 20)
1 cup plus 2 tablespoons dry couscous
seeds of 1 medium pomegranate
²/₃ cup shelled pistachios (roasted or unroasted)
6 tablespoons coarsely chopped cilantro
6 tablespoons coarsely chopped mint
zest of 1 lemon, removed with a zester
1 tablespoon lemon juice
4 tablespoons extra virgin olive oil
pomegranate syrup, to serve (optional)

In a small saucepan, bring the stock to a boil, season with salt, if you wish, and add the saffron. Pour this over the couscous in a large bowl, cover, and set aside for 30 minutes, stirring and breaking it up halfway through. Let the couscous cool completely.

Mix the pomegranate seeds, pistachios, herbs, and lemon zest into the couscous. You can prepare the salad to this point in advance and transport it in a sealed container. In a small sealable container to transport, whisk the lemon juice with the olive oil and some salt. At the picnic, pour the dressing over the salad, toss, and drizzle with pomegranate syrup.

Kit Serving spoon, plate, fork

SUNDAY ROAST PICNIC

It's easy to picture rural scenes of

meadows and riverbanks when you think of a picnic, but cities offer myriad places too. Most cities around the world have parks—big open spaces landscaped for our pleasure, with grass just waiting for us to come along with a blanket under our arm. In fact, because of the nature of land ownership in some countries, urban areas can offer many more opportunities for picnics and lovely walks than the countryside does. Whichever city of the world you happen to find yourself in, an escape from the hustle and bustle of the sidewalks is never far away.

So, this chapter lies particularly close to my heart, given how much time we spend in London. In fact, this is my Hyde Park ideal; being able to spread yourself on blankets in the shade of a plane tree somewhere between the Round Pond and the Serpentine, and you have an afternoon of hippy nirvana without leaving town. Opening up a foil pouch with a roast chicken still slightly warm from the oven, for eating with some crisp green leaves and a loaf of coarsely torn sourdough bread or a baguette, and it is about as close as it gets to heaven in my book.

In fact, a Sunday roast picnic is rather easier than going the whole hog of a roast lunch at home, where there are all those trimmings to consider and pans to wash at the end. Come the summer we can forego all of that and turn to relaxed Mediterranean flavors and vegetables, with bread taking the place of potatoes. The idea is to get roasting while packing (or the other way around), then whisk your chicken, leg of lamb, or the like straight from the oven, wrapped in its foil overcoat, hot to your destination, where it will still have that gorgeous ambient succulence that belongs to meat by rights before it has been cooled or chilled.

There is something deliciously decadent about eating slightly warm or freshly cooked food out of doors, just as swimming in a steaming hot swimming pool in the freezing cold has an air of being exotic. Removed from their normal setting, the humblest of roasts seems special.

Getting in there with your fingers adds to the charming, lovely messy rusticity, so I wouldn't even think knife and fork here. The meat drippings are at the ready for mopping up with a hunk of bread—a twenty-first century tale of bread and drippings, something my mother's generation regarded as a treat long after the war was over and butter was back on the menu.

"There is something deliciously decadent about eating slightly warm or freshly cooked food out of doors."

LET'S GO: ROASTS

As a last-minute solution to a picnic, I am more likely to roast a chicken or cook some sausage than anything else. Recently I had to put this to the ultimate test, when the chicken I had lined up for fifteen of us for a Sunday lunch picnic proved to be less than fresh on the morning. So, the challenge was to get to the store, get home, roast a main dish, and get to the picnic all in the space of an hour and a half. And it worked! A row of chickens roasted with ras al hanout were hot and on the blanket in time. If you line the roasting pan with a double thickness of foil large enough to wrap the bird up in as it comes out of the oven, it should still be slightly warm a couple of hours later.

AROUND THE WORLD IN 80 SAUSAGES

I swear by roasting **sausage** in the oven, where they caramelize beautifully and evenly; in fact, I cannot recall the last time I cooked one in a skillet—too messy by half. Different types and sizes will inevitably differ marginally in the length of time they take to cook, but as a rule of thumb, lay them out in a roasting pan spaced slightly apart (you can brush it with **vegetable oil** first if wished, although I don't usually bother). Then roast for 35 to 40 minutes at 425°F, turning them once with a spatula.

A SALT AND PEPPER BIRD

A salt and pepper bird is just that—a sprinkling of **sea salt** and grinding of **black pepper**; there is enough fat beneath the skin to baste it. Roast a **3½-pound free-range untrussed bird** for 50 to 55 minutes at 425°F, until the skin is golden and the juices run clear when a knife is inserted into the thigh.
For 4 to 5 people

GARLIC AND THYME CHICKEN

Coat a **3½-pound free-range untrussed chicken** with **olive oil** and season it with **sea salt** and **black pepper**, then pop some **thyme**, a smashed **garlic clove or two**, and **half an onion** into the cavity and roast as opposite.
For 4 to 5 people

BUTTER AND LEMON CHICKEN

Another favorite way is to dot a **3½-pound free-range untrussed chicken** with **unsalted butter**, then squeeze over a bit of **lemon juice** (popping the squeezed-out lemon inside), season it well with **sea salt** and **black pepper**, and roast as opposite.
For 4 to 5 people

SPICY ROAST CHICKEN

In a small bowl, mix 1 teaspoon of **ras al hanout or garam masala** with 1 tablespoon of **lemon juice** and 2 tablespoons of **olive oil**. Smear this over a **3½-pound free-range untrussed chicken** on a plate. If you like you can chill it for a couple of hours. Season with **sea salt** and **black pepper** and roast as opposite.
For 4 to 5 people

MY FAVORITE PICNIC ROAST CHICKEN

This is my default bird, scented with resinous herbs and with lots of lemony juices to mop up with a hunk of bread or some green leaves.

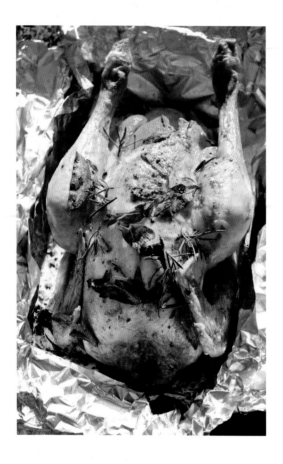

For 6 people

one approx. 3½-pound free-range chicken,
  untrussed
sea salt and black pepper
a large handful of sage leaves and a few
  rosemary sprigs
3 tablespoons extra virgin olive oil
1 lemon, halved

Preheat the oven to 425°F. Place the chicken in a roasting pan lined with a double thickness of foil large enough to wrap the bird up in once cooked —depending on the width of the foil, you may find it easiest to place the sheets at right angles to each other.

Season the chicken and scatter over the sage leaves and rosemary sprigs, first pulling off half the needles. Carefully drizzle over the oil, taking care not to dislodge the herbs, squeeze over the juice of a lemon, and pop the squeezed-out halves inside the chicken. Roast for 1 hour, then skim off the excess fat from the drippings and wrap up in the foil to transport.

Kit Sharp knife, plate, knife and fork (optional)

GORGEOUSLY BUTTERY VERY FRENCH CHICKEN

The herbs that go to make up a classical French "fines herbes" together form one of the quintessential scents of the cooking of this country. But finding fresh chervil? I confess that I have hardly ever seen it outside of doing time as a commis chef in a restaurant. There is no real substitute, but if needs must, then mock up its gentle shades of tarragon in parsley with a bit of the former and more of the latter—that is, a blend of tarragon, parsley, and chives. Whatever route you choose—and you could even reduce it to parsley alone—this is still a brilliant way of cooking chicken, its flesh infused with buttery succulence and a rich skin.

For 4 people

5 tablespoons finely chopped herbs, such as
    chervil, tarragon, chives, parsley
1/3 cup unsalted butter, softened
sea salt and black pepper
one 3½-pound free-range chicken, untrussed

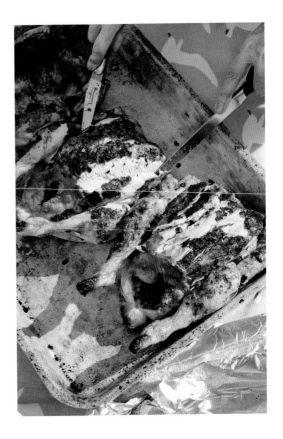

Preheat the oven to 425°F. In a bowl, beat the herbs with 4 tablespoons of the butter and half a teaspoon each of salt and pepper. Starting at the neck end of the chicken, slip your fingers beneath the skin to loosen it over each breast. Gently smooth the butter and herb mixture over the breasts and pat the skin back into place, spreading the butter out evenly. Rub the remaining butter over the chicken and season.

Place the chicken in a roasting pan that holds it quite snugly, lined with a double thickness of foil large enough to wrap the chicken up in—depending on the width of the foil, you may find it easiest to place two sheets at right angles to each other. Roast for 50 minutes, then spoon off any excess fat in the bottom of the pan and wrap up in the foil to transport.

Kit Sharp knife, plate, knife and fork (optional)

CHICKEN TIKKA MASALA

Despite having to do a bit of cooking, this marinade won't take more than 10 minutes to make. It can be whipped up the night before and the chicken left to marinate, ready to cook when you need it. One of the speedy dips such as guacamole (see page 30) or tzatziki (see page 30) make a good addition here, or an eggplant or roasted bell pepper one. Alternatively, take a cucumber to slice when you get there for assembling tikka sandwiches.

Makes 12 mini tikkas

6 skinless chicken breasts (approx. 1½ to 1¾ pounds)
Tikka marinade
peanut or vegetable oil
1 onion, peeled and finely chopped
3 garlic cloves, peeled and crushed to a paste
2-inch piece fresh ginger, peeled and grated or finely chopped

1 teaspoon yellow mustard seeds
½ teaspoon ground cumin or seeds
1 teaspoon garam masala
½ teaspoon cayenne pepper
⅓ cup plus 1 tablespoon tomato paste
sea salt
⅔ cup coconut milk
coarsely chopped cilantro, to serve

Make the marinade: In a large skillet, heat a couple of tablespoons of oil over medium heat, add the onion, and sauté for a few minutes, until softened and starting to color, stirring occasionally. Add the garlic and ginger and cook for another minute or so, stirring frequently. Now stir in the spices and cook briefly until fragrant. Stir in the tomato paste, season with salt, and cook for another minute or so, then gradually stir in the coconut milk. Transfer the marinade to a large container and let cool. You can prepare this the night before your picnic.

Cut out the white tendon on the underside of each chicken breast if evident, and halve into two long strips. Coat the breasts with the marinade in the bowl, cover, and chill or let stand in a cool place for a couple of hours or overnight.

Heat a ridged grill pan over high heat. The chicken breasts should be lightly coated in the marinade. Drizzle a bit of oil over either side and grill until striped with gold and cooked through, a few minutes each side—you can press down with spatula for this bit, and they should feel firm. Scatter with cilantro before packaging to transport to your picnic.

Kit Plate, knife and fork

BAKED CHICKEN WITH ZA'ATAR AND PINE NUTS

You should end up here with a delectable pool of juices, sharpened with lemon and scented with cinnamon and the thyme of the za'atar (online at www.kalustyans.com), though almost any Middle Eastern spice blend can be used, so tailor it to fit the pantry. The pine nuts and cilantro are a frill—if I am catering for lots of children, then I tend to leave these aside as an option for those that want.

For 6 people

2 lemons
²/₃ cup extra virgin olive oil
3 garlic cloves, peeled and crushed to a paste
1 red onion, peeled and finely chopped
2 heaping teaspoons za'atar
2 cinnamon sticks, broken in half
4 to 4½ pounds chicken thighs and drumsticks
sea salt and black pepper
¹/₃ cup pine nuts (optional)
cilantro leaves, to serve (optional)

Slice one of the lemons, discarding the ends, and juice the other. In a large bowl, combine the lemon juice and olive oil, garlic, onion, za'atar, cinnamon, and sliced lemon. Add the chicken pieces to the bowl and coat with the marinade. Cover and chill for several hours.

Preheat the oven to 425°F. Season the chicken parts and arrange them skin-side up in a single layer in two roasting pans, drizzling over the marinade and tucking the lemon slices between them. Bake for 35 minutes, until golden, scattering over the pine nuts, if including, after 15 minutes. Skim off the excess fat and package to transport. A few cilantro leaves scattered over before serving is a lively touch.

Kit Serving plate

MUSTARD ROAST GUINEA FOWL QUARTERS

Guinea fowl tend to come up that little bit smaller than chicken, which makes them good for eating in quarters. But they do call for a knife and fork, being that much firmer than a chicken. If buying from a butcher, then I would prevail upon them to cut the birds up for you, but otherwise it's a fairly straightforward task, but a strong pair of hands is required.

For 6 people

two 2½ to 2¾-pound guinea fowl, quartered
3 tablespoons cider vinegar
approx. 6 tablespoons peanut oil
1½ pounds red onions, peeled and quartered or
    cut into slim wedges, depending on their size
approx. 10 bay leaves
sea salt and black pepper
1 tablespoon Dijon mustard
1 level tablespoon savory or thyme leaves

Place the guinea fowl parts in a large bowl, pour over the vinegar and a couple of tablespoons of oil, cover, and let marinate in a cool place for an hour, or chill.

Preheat the oven to 425°F. Arrange the guinea fowl parts skin-side-up in two roasting pans surrounded by the onions and bay leaves so that they sit in a crowded single layer. Pour the marinade over the contents, drizzle over another 2 to 3 tablespoons of oil, and season, then roast for 20 minutes.

Give the onions a stir, brush the guinea fowl pieces with the mustard, and scatter over the savory or thyme. Baste the meat with any drippings and drizzle over another tablespoon or so of oil, then return to the oven for another 15 to 20 minutes. Pour off the drippings, skim off the fat, and serve the remainder drizzled over the guinea fowl and onions.

Kit Plate, knife and fork (optional)

LEG OF LAMB WITH ANCHOVIES

HERBED RACK OF LAMB

Roast lamb studded with anchovies is one of those strange but true combinations, where it brings out the sweetness of the flesh yet there is no hint of the salty little fish; they simply melt away. A small leg weighing 3½ to 3¾ pounds is perfect for four (although obviously you can roast a larger one).

Delicate pale pink chops are perfect for nibbling in hand at a slightly special picnic. Either slice them just before you go, and keep the rack together wrapped in foil, or, as they cut like butter, take a sharp folding knife and do it when you arrive at your picnic location.

For 4 people

one approx. 3¾-pound leg of lamb, shank removed
4 to 5 salted anchovies, cut into ½-inch pieces
extra virgin olive oil
sea salt and black pepper
a handful of thyme sprigs

For 6 people

sea salt and black pepper
two 18-ounce to 25-ounce racks of lamb
2 teaspoons whole grain mustard
several handfuls each of sage and bay leaves, and rosemary sprigs
extra virgin olive oil

Preheat the oven to 475°F. Using a sharp knife, make slits all over the lamb flesh and, with the help of the tip of a teaspoon handle, insert a piece of anchovy into each one. Drizzle some olive oil all over the lamb, season the roast, and place fat-side up in a roasting pan that holds it snugly, on top of the thyme. You can also tuck the shank bone under the edge of the joint.

Roast for 15 minutes, then turn the oven down to 350°F and cook for another 55 minutes (cook for 15 minutes per pound for medium). Wrap in foil and you're ready to go. Carve the lamb across the grain—you may prefer to do this just before you leave the house, in which case let rest for 15 to 20 minutes first.

Preheat the oven to 425°F. Heat a large skillet over medium-high heat, season the racks of lamb, and color the fat-side one at a time. Once browned, brush a teaspoon of mustard over the fat of each one.

Scatter some of the herbs over the bottom of a roasting pan lined with a double thickness of foil large enough to wrap the lamb up in once cooked. Drizzle over a bit of oil, place the racks fat-side up on top, then scatter over some more herbs and drizzle over some more oil. Roast for about 30 minutes to leave them medium–rare. Wrap up to transport.

Kit Sharp knife, plate, knife and fork (optional)

Kit Sharp knife, plate, knife and fork (optional)

RARE ROAST BEEF WITH BALSAMIC BELL PEPPERS

A rare beef roast comes high on my list for a glam picnic, dressed up with roasted vegetables. You could add in a runny goat cheese, some olives, and other Mediterranean frills that will keep it in picnic mode. When the French take such a roast on a picnic, they drizzle it with oil as a finishing touch, but the Cheat's Aioli (see page 30) is a perfect match. You may find it easiest to carve this roast before leaving the house, but do it as close to the picnic time as possible, and then wrap it up tightly in foil.

This slow-roasting method enhances the natural tenderness of the meat. The bell peppers obviously turn it into a more complete event, but should you simply want a lovely beef roast on its own, sear and then cook the meat in a large skillet with a heatproof handle over high heat. Roast the beef in the skillet for 50 minutes to leave it rare.

For 6 people

Beef
extra virgin olive oil
one approx. 3-pound rolled beef top round or
   top loin roast
1 scant teaspoon English mustard powder
sea salt and black pepper
1 heaping tablespoon whole grain mustard

Bell peppers
4 red bell peppers, cores and seeds removed
   and cut into strips 1¼ to 1½-inch wide
2 red onions, peeled and cut into thin wedges
2 bay leaves
extra virgin olive oil
2 tablespoons balsamic vinegar

Preheat the oven to 300°F. In a large skillet, heat about a teaspoon of oil over high heat. Using a tea strainer, dust the roast all over with the mustard powder and season it. Sear on all four sides, and the ends, until golden; it should be well-colored as you're roasting at a fairly low temperature. Brush half the whole grain mustard over the bottom of the roast using a pastry brush, and the rest over the top.

Arrange the peppers, onions, and bay leaves in a large roasting pan, drizzle over 3 tablespoons of oil, season, and nestle the beef in the center. Roast the beef for 1 hour, or until it registers approximately 113°F in the center using a meat thermometer (for rare). Transfer it to a plate or wrap in foil to transport.

Turn the oven up to 450°F, drizzle half the balsamic vinegar over the peppers and onions, and stir, then continue to roast for 10 to 20 minutes, until golden and syrupy. Drizzle over the remaining tablespoon of balsamic vinegar and stir. Thinly carve the beef and serve with the peppers.

Kit Sharp knife, plate, knife and fork (optional)

EGGPLANT VEGGIE ROAST WITH GOAT CHEESE AND TOMATOES

Roasted eggplant slices, crisp on the outside and deliciously succulent within, piled up with tomatoes and goat cheese make an excellent veggie picnic roast.

For 6 people

3 eggplants, sliced approx. 1¼-inch thick,
   ends discarded
extra virgin olive oil
sea salt and black pepper

2 cups cherry tomatoes, halved or quartered,
   depending on size
5½ ounces young firm goat cheese, cut into
   approx. ½-inch dice
coarsely chopped flat-leaf parsley

Preheat the oven to 425°F. Lay the eggplant slices out on a couple of cookie sheets, with a bit of space between each slice. Brush the slices with oil on both sides and season the top. Roast for 20 minutes, then turn them and cook until golden, another 15 to 20 minutes. At the same time, place the tomatoes in a bowl, scatter a bit of salt over them, and set aside.

Transfer the eggplant slices to a large roasting pan that holds them in a single layer with a bit of space in between. Pour 3 tablespoons of oil over the tomatoes and gently toss, then mix in the goat cheese. Pile this on top of the eggplant slices and return to the oven for 4 to 5 minutes to warm through, then let cool. Scatter with lots of chopped parsley. Transport in the roasting pan covered with foil, or transfer to a plate or container and cover.

Kit Serving spoon, plate, knife and fork

VITELLO TONNATO

For extra-special occasions, vitello tonnato never fails to please. Your best bet here is a top round roast.

For 6 people

Veal
1 teaspoon extra virgin olive oil
sea salt and black pepper
one 2-pound boneless veal top round roast
1 small onion, peeled, halved, and sliced
a couple of rosemary sprigs
²/₃ cup white wine

Sauce
1 medium organic egg yolk
half 5-ounce can tuna in spring water, drained
4 salted anchovy fillets
1 cup olive oil, or ²/₃ cup extra virgin olive oil
   and ¹/₃ cup peanut oil
1 tablespoon lemon juice
a jar of capers, and of salted anchovies, to serve

Preheat the oven to 300°F. In a large skillet, heat the oil over high heat. Season the veal with salt and pepper and sear on all sides until well colored. Place the veal in a roasting pan that will hold it snugly on top of the onion and rosemary. Pour the wine into the bottom. Cover with foil and roast for about 1 hour, or until a meat thermometer reaches 131 to 140°F inserted into the center of the thickest section (for medium-rare) and it feels soft when pressed—start checking it after about 50 minutes. Transfer the veal to a plate, cover with foil, and let cool. Slice the veal wafer thin and wrap in foil.

Strain the pan drippings and use them in the sauce. Make the sauce: In a food processor, blitz the egg yolk, tuna, and anchovies to a paste. Slowly incorporate half of the oil with the motor running as though making a mayonnaise, scraping down the side as you go if necessary. Add the lemon juice, then incorporate the remaining oil and about 4 tablespoons of the veal drippings, which will be more or less all of it—you should have a rich pouring sauce. Serve the veal coated with the sauce, with some capers and an anchovy fillet on the side.

Kit Serving spoon, plate, knife and fork

GRAND SALMON

As fashions change, this dish has the same appeal as the whole poached salmon of yesteryear. A fish this size makes a big but an affordable splash, especially if you buy a good farmed salmon.

For 10 people

2 tablespoons each of finely chopped dill, chives, and flat-leaf parsley
1 teaspoon fennel seeds, coarsely ground
sea salt and black pepper
one approx. 6½-pound salmon, cleaned and scaled, head and tail removed
4 tablespoons extra virgin olive oil
juice of 1 lemon
3 tablespoons white wine

Caper Mayonnaise
¾ heaping cup mayonnaise
a squeeze of lemon juice and ½ teaspoon finely grated lemon zest
2 tablespoons capers, rinsed and coarsely chopped

In a bowl or container, beat all the ingredients together. Cover and chill or keep in a cool place.

Preheat the oven to 425°F and preheat the broiler. Combine the herbs and fennel seeds with a teaspoon of salt and about the same amount of black pepper.

Score the salmon flesh diagonally on both sides at 2-inch intervals with deep slits and season the fish with salt and pepper. Lay a double thickness of foil on top of your broiler pan so that it is a bit longer than the fish. Lay the salmon on top, cupping the edges of the foil, and broil one side until the skin blisters and colors, 3 to 4 minutes. Then stuff half of the herbs into the slits, turn, and repeat with the other side.

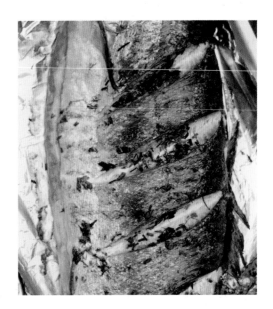

Pour over the olive oil, lemon juice, and wine and roast, uncovered, for 40 to 45 minutes. Check whether the fish is cooked by slipping a sharp knife between the backbone and the flesh. The flesh should easily lift off the bones; if it clings or looks translucent, then it needs a bit longer. You can fillet the fish before going, in which case let cool.

Kit Sharp knife, serving spoon, plate, knife and fork

HOT FOOD
ON LOCATION

Some of my fondest memories of

picnics revolve around what can at best be described as dodgy weather. Lighting fires on blustery Hebridean beaches, buttoned to the chin and shivering, huddling around a stack of smoking logs, and grilling scallops or hot dogs in between sandcastle and dam-building duty is a parental rite of passage, and a fine lunch at the end is a great reward. Food doesn't get much better or tastier than in those kind of circumstances, so it's worth every heave of the shovel.

That said, there is dodgy and there is dodgy; and a spell—however brief—of sunshine works wonders for any occasion. Searing heatwaves, however, that leave you wishing you could stay in the car when you get there to take advantage of the AC are by no means the best time to be packing up with a view to taking off for lunch. Not least because you will need to find shade when you arrive; there is only so much that sunblock and floppy hats can do. So, a windswept beach, an autumnal wood, or meadowscape at Easter, beautiful if chilly, can make for truly lovely outdoor gatherings. The foil to this, if we want to be exceptionally civilized, is something warming along the way. And even if it isn't chilly (do we really need an excuse?), I love picnics that mix it up, some grilled food thrown in with the usual

spread, and the offer of a small cup of soup to begin is unlikely to result in rejection.

This is where small traveling charcoal grills come into their own. They can be preloaded with briquettes and firelighters at home, ready for lighting at the strike of a match. Cooking on a picnic may find us less well-prepared than when we are camping—that bijou kitchen-in-a-box begins to seem like a luxury when you have no water, no cutting board, and no knives. So, the answer is to have absolutely everything done at home before you go. Get whatever it is you are cooking ready as far as is humanly possible in an airtight container, at the ready for grilling.

Alternatively, fast forward to a dank and drizzly day, walking in the woods kicking through damp leaves or the long wet grasses of an orchard after a spring shower. We might play this slightly differently to our summer picnics—out goes the basket and in comes a backpack or shoulder bag, and a coat is as good as a blanket for sitting on. The chances are we don't want to sit around, but rest and recharge. Again, think of the pleasurable promise of a thermos of steaming hot soup that can be poured into mugs to revive numbing fingers as well as doing that oatmeal-like thing of heating you from the inside out.

"A windswept beach, an autumnal wood, or meadowscape at Easter, beautiful if chilly, can make for truly lovely outdoor gatherings."

FOOD IN A THERMOS

REAL OATMEAL WITH WHISKEY

However beautiful the morning, there will almost certainly be a nip in the air, and maybe a dew if it's a lovely summer's day. The best oatmeal splutters away for some 20 minutes—it's worth going to the trouble of cooking this with old-fashioned rolled oats. To be truly decadent, take a small jar of brown sugar, a hip flask of whiskey, and a small pot of cream.

For 4 people

2 cups rolled oats
5 cups water
½ teaspoon sea salt

light brown sugar, whiskey,
and heavy cream, to serve

Place the oats, water, and salt in a saucepan (ideally, a nonstick one) and bring to a boil over high heat, stirring continuously. Reduce the heat to low and continue to cook until the oatmeal is swollen and thickened, about 25 minutes, stirring occasionally.

The oatmeal will be thinner than you would normally make it, allowing for it to firm up in the thermos. Pour it into a food or wide-necked thermos. Give it a stir before dishing up with sugar, whiskey for those that want, and plenty of cream.

Kit Long spoon for stirring, bowls or cups, spoons

ROAST TOMATO SOUP

Soups don't get any simpler than this, or tomato soups much better or more vibrant. Quite simply, it's a magical concoction of tomatoes, onions, and olive oil. No stock is required; the roasting does for that as well as bringing out the flavor of the vegetables at the same time.

For 6 people

5 pounds tomatoes, left on the vine
3 red onions, peeled, and cut into wedges
extra virgin olive oil
sea salt and black pepper
celery salt
1½ teaspoons sugar

Preheat the oven to 450°F. Arrange the tomatoes and onions in a couple of large roasting pans in a single layer, drizzle over 5 tablespoons of oil, and roast for 20 minutes. Let cool.

Once they are cool enough to handle, pinch the tomatoes off the vines using a fork, and transfer to a blender with the onions and roasting juices. Add a good dose of salt, some celery salt, some black pepper, the sugar, and another 5 tablespoons of oil, then blend. Pass through a strainer into a saucepan and gently reheat before pouring into a thermos.

Kit Cups or bowls, spoons

SPICY BUTTERNUT SQUASH SOUP

Have some fun here and experiment with squashes and pumpkins you might not normally buy. Butternut squash promises to be the sweetest of all, but you can always add a bit of sugar if you feel the call is there.

For 6 people

4 tablespoons unsalted butter
1 large onion, peeled and chopped
2 tablespoons chopped fresh ginger
two 2-pound butternut squash, skinned, seeded, and coarsely chopped
1 quart fresh vegetable or chicken stock
sea salt and black pepper
2/3 cup crème fraîche
freshly grated nutmeg

In a large saucepan, melt the butter over medium heat, add the onion, ginger, and squash, and cook until glossy, about 5 minutes, stirring frequently. Add the stock and plenty of seasoning, pressing the squash down to submerge it, bring to a boil, and simmer until the squash is tender, 10 to 15 minutes. Blend the soup in batches in a blender with the crème fraîche and a generous grating of nutmeg, then pass it through a strainer. Gently reheat before transferring to a thermos.

Kit Cups or bowls, spoons

FRENCH ONION SOUP

The earthy and gutsy character of French onion soup makes it ideal cockle-warming stuff. The dash of brandy at the end requires a hip flask of the liquor, which will, of course, need finishing off before you return in order to lighten the load, making for a merry time on a chilly day. Large paper cups or bowls are ideal here, as you can put the shredded cheese into the bottom and stack them before you leave, ready to receive the hot soup from a thermos, with no dishwashing to follow.

For 4 people

4 tablespoons unsalted butter
3 onions, peeled, halved, and thinly sliced
2/3 cup white wine
3¾ cups chicken stock
sea salt and black pepper
2/3 cup shredded Gruyère
2 tablespoons brandy (optional)
crusty bread, to serve

In a large saucepan, melt the butter over medium heat and cook the onions until a deep even gold, 20 to 30 minutes, stirring frequently. It's really important to take your time here and not rush. Add the wine and simmer until well reduced, then add the chicken stock and some seasoning, bring to a boil, and simmer over low heat for 10 minutes. The soup can be made in advance, in which case reheat and pour boiling hot into a wide-necked thermos.

Divide the Gruyère between four cups (you can do this before leaving home if you like). Pour the hot soup over and add a bit of brandy, if wished. Serve with bread.

Kit Cups or bowls, spoons

MEATBALL AND BEAN CASSEROLE

A really rustic soup, the sausage plays the role of meatballs that get wolfed down, and there are enough cans involved to ensure it isn't too arduous.

For 6 people

1 to 2 tablespoons extra virgin olive oil

8 small pork sausages, skinned and thickly sliced

4½ ounces chorizo, raw or cooked, halved and sliced ½-inch thick

2 onions, peeled and chopped

1 celery heart, trimmed and sliced

½ small head of savoy cabbage, finely sliced and cut into 1½ to 2-inch lengths

²/₃ cup white wine

one 14.5-ounce can diced tomatoes

one 15-ounce can chickpeas (garbanzo beans), drained and rinsed

one 14-ounce can flageolet or haricot beans, drained and rinsed

1 quart chicken stock

sea salt

a pinch of dried red pepper flakes

2 large handfuls of coarsely chopped flat-leaf parsley, plus extra to serve

In a large saucepan, heat a tablespoon of oil over medium heat and pan-fry all the sausage until lightly colored, 5 to 10 minutes, carefully turning with a spatula now and again. Transfer them to a bowl.

If necessary add another tablespoon of oil to the pan, but there should be plenty given out by the sausage, and sauté the onion and celery until golden and glossy, 10 to 15 minutes, stirring occasionally. Add the cabbage and cook until wilted, several minutes, then add the wine and tomatoes and simmer to reduce by half. Return the sausage to the pan, add the chickpeas and beans, the stock, plenty of salt, and the red pepper flakes. Bring to a boil and simmer for 10 minutes.

Taste for seasoning and stir in the parsley, though you could also take this separately to add just before eating, if wished. Transfer to a food thermos.

Kit Cups or bowls, spoons

GRILLS

Nothing that follows by way of grills, I promise, is going to take you more than 10 minutes before you start. One of the pluses of having a grill on location has to be that you can call on it when you don't have time even for the usual half hour or so in the kitchen to rustle up some salads or sandwiches. These grills are designed to be "shop and go."

My favorite travel grill hasn't changed since we wrote *The Camping Cookbook*. The bijoux Weber Smokey Joe gets my vote every time, not least because it comes with a lid (see page 16); although if you are grilling without a lid, then it is worth keeping a water spray to hand to quell any flareups.

Beyond this, Top Tip number 1 has to be to remember to get your coals really hot before you start grilling. The timings given on a package of briquettes have a habit of looking on the bright side. If it says they heat up in 20 minutes, you can count on a good hour before they will be covered in that desirable fine layer of white ash that's so important to good results. And here especially, where the foods are all fast-cooking by design, that heat is all important.

Top Tip number 2 is to throw away that half bag of briquettes from last summer, if it happens to be the first barbecue of the season. If it's been sitting in a shed or garage, there is every chance they will be damp and never get properly hot. I hope that by putting this in writing I will actually start to follow my own advice on this one. I habitually forget over the winter.

Weber Smokey Joe

"By having a grill on location, you can call on it when you don't have time for the half hour in the kitchen to rustle up some salads or sandwiches."

TRAVELER'S CROQUE MONSIEUR

Traveling around France in search of a decent Croque Monsieur becomes an increasingly dispiriting business. In fact, it's hard to believe such a simple creation can have become so warped by the need for convenience. The fact we search at all is that there is no toasted sandwich to beat it—there is something magical about that crisp toasted cushion oozing nutty Gruyère laced with Dijon mustard, and a thick slice of baked ham, and you are guaranteed the finest results if you make them yourself. The good news is that they can be assembled well in advance, and they travel.

For 2 people

unsalted butter, softened for spreading
4½-inch slices coarse-textured white bread,
    such as pain de Campagne
7 ounces Gruyère, thinly sliced
2 to 4 slices honey-baked ham
Dijon mustard

AT HOME
Butter the bread on both sides. Cover two of the slices with a layer of Gruyère, then a layer of ham, smear over some mustard, and cover with another layer of Gruyère. Close the sandwiches with the top layers of bread. They can be prepared to this point in advance, in which case, wrap in plastic wrap and chill until you're ready to go.

ON LOCATION
Toast the sandwiches on the outside of the grill, turning them around now and again so that they toast evenly, until golden and crisp and the cheese within has melted, 2 to 4 minutes each side. Cut the toasted sandwiches in half for eating with napkins.

Kit Charcoal grill (preloaded with briquettes, firelighters, matches), spatula, sharp knife, serving plate, napkins

SAUSAGE SPLITS

Could this be the answer to avoiding burned sausage? By slitting the sausage open, you halve the thickness, cutting down on the time needed to grill them. And the insides cook to that especially alluring caramelized finish usually found in the bits that burst out from sausage as it cooks.

For 6 people

6 pork sausages
6 hot dog buns
3 tablespoons sour cream
3 tablespoons mayonnaise

2 teaspoons Dijon mustard
baby leaves and cocktail gherkins, rinsed and
    halved lengthwise, to serve

AT HOME
Slit the sausage lengthwise and open out so that they are evenly thick. Slit the rolls open, leaving them attached at the side. In a sealable bowl or container, beat together the sour cream, mayonnaise, and mustard. Wrap the sausage and rolls in foil.

ON LOCATION
Grill the sausage for 4 to 5 minutes each side, skin side-down first, which will set the cut surface on top. Briefly toast the buns on either side. Place a sausage in each open bun, pile with some leaves, drizzle over the sauce, and adorn with a few cocktail gherkins.

Kit Charcoal grill (preloaded with briquettes, firelighters, matches), tongs

BASIL BURGERS

I once managed to horrify a family member, who was kindly babysitting, by suggesting that she made the children some hamburgers for supper. "Ground meat, chopped shallot, salt and pepper, and shape into a disk," I explained, to assuage her appalled expression. "Well, I doubt I'll go to the trouble of chopping a shallot," she replied. But yes, it really is that simple, even if I have taken the liberty of adding a bit of basil here and some sumac—the ground rust-red berries that have traditionally replaced lemon in the mountainous regions of Lebanon. You can also make delicious kofta burgers. Simply combine the lamb with 1 ounce each of finely chopped **cilantro** and **flat-leaf parsley** (leaves and fine stalks), 1 small peeled and finely chopped **onion**, ¼ teaspoon **cayenne**, and a teaspoon of **cumin** and of **sea salt**.

For 4 people/Makes 8 mini-burgers

1¾ ounces basil leaves
2 shallots, peeled
1 teaspoon sumac
1 garlic clove, peeled
sea salt and black pepper
extra virgin olive oil
21 ounces ground lamb
pita breads, hummus, and cilantro sprigs,
    to serve

AT HOME

In a food processor, process all the ingredients for the burgers except for the lamb with 1 tablespoon of olive oil to a coarse purée. In a large bowl, mix the purée with the lamb, then form into eight burgers. These can be made in advance; if so, cover and chill them.

ON LOCATION

Grill the burgers over a hot grill until golden brown and firm when pressed, a few minutes each side. They find a natural home in a warm pita pocket with a dollop of hummus and a few cilantro leaves.

Kit Charcoal grill (preloaded with briquettes, firelighters, matches), tongs, sharp knife

LEMON CHICKEN FILLETS WITH CRISPY BACON

Chicken marinated with lemon and eaten with a slice of crispy bacon makes a fabulous picnic lineup. The temptation to add in some flat-leaf parsley (something my husband says I use far too much of) is almost too hard to resist, but over to you on that one. Just a bit at the end perhaps. I would serve them slipped inside pita pockets or with a green or tomato salad.

For 4 people

4 skinless chicken cutlets (approx. 18 to
   21 ounces)
finely grated zest and juice of 1 lemon
5 tablespoons extra virgin olive oil

sea salt and black pepper
4 unsmoked bacon slices
coarsely chopped flat-leaf parsley, to serve
   (optional)

AT HOME
Cut out the white tendon on the underside of the chicken fillets, if visible. In an airtight sealable container, whisk together the lemon zest, juice, and olive oil. Add the chicken fillets, toss to coat, and put on the lid.

ON LOCATION
Season the chicken and grill until golden and firm when pressed, 5 to 7 minutes each side. Grill the bacon on both sides for 3 to 4 minutes in total (if there is room on the grill, this can be done at the same time as the chicken).

Drizzle some of the marinade over the chicken, top with a sliver of bacon, and scatter over some parsley, if wished.

Kit Charcoal grill (preloaded with briquettes, firelighters, matches), tongs, sharp knife

JEAN-CHRISTOPHE'S CHICKEN WINGS

The reputation of these chicken wings follows in the wake of their creator Jean-Christophe Chavaillard, a larger-than-life Norman restaurateur whose former domaine Equinoxe suggests the spirit within—a bar on one side frequented by salty old sea-dogs, and women in faded Lanvin scarves inevitably accompanied by a "monsieur d'un certain age" filling the tables of the dining salon. Moules and huîtres floated between the two, bridging the cultural divide, and everyone got along famously. Sadly, such was his success that he then moved to a bigger, better bar and dining salon overlooking the Baie du Mont Saint Michel. I had the good fortune to acquire the secret of his sticky chicken wings before he left.

Makes 12

Marinade
4 tablespoons extra virgin olive oil
1 tablespoon finely chopped rosemary
1 tablespoon finely chopped thyme
2 bay leaves, torn into pieces
3 garlic cloves, peeled and crushed to a paste
Chicken
12 chicken wings
1 tablespoon Dijon mustard
1 tablespoon honey
sea salt and black pepper

AT HOME

In a large bowl, combine all the ingredients for the marinade. Add the chicken wings and coat them, then cover and chill overnight.

In a small bowl, mix the mustard with the honey. Turn the wings in their marinade and season.

ON LOCATION

Grill the wings until they seem half-cooked and mid-gold, 10 to 20 minutes, turning them once and moving them around as necessary. Brush on both sides with the mustard–honey glaze and cook until golden and cooked through, approximately 10 minutes more, again turning them once.

Kit Charcoal grill (preloaded with briquettes, firelighters, matches), tongs

MINTY LAMB CHOPS WITH ZUCCHINI

If you can't quite leave weekend lamb roast with mint sauce behind, then give this outdoor take on it a whirl. Zucchini always grill up a treat, turning gorgeously sweet in the throes of cooking, which takes care of meat and one veggie. Some ripe tomatoes would, as ever, be lovely here too.

For 4 people

2 teaspoons mint sauce
a squeeze of lemon juice
sea salt and black pepper
6 tablespoons extra virgin olive oil

10½ ounces zucchini, ends discarded and
  sliced lengthwise
6 lamb chops, ¾ to 1¼-inch thick

AT HOME

In a small sealable container, whisk the mint sauce, lemon juice, and a bit of salt with 4 tablespoons of olive oil until amalgamated. Place the zucchini slices in a another sealable container with the remaining olive oil and some seasoning, then put on the lid and turn it a few times to coat the zucchini.

ON LOCATION

Season the lamb chops and grill until golden and firm but with a slight give when pressed, 3 to 4 minutes each side. Transfer to a plate and cover with foil, if you have some. Grill the zucchini slices for a few minutes each side—the first side may take a bit longer. Serve the chops and zucchini slices with the mint dressing spooned over.

Kit Charcoall grill (preloaded with briquettes, firelighters, matches), plate, foil, knife and fork (optional)

STEAK WITH GARLIC BUTTER

A whizzy garlic butter with watercress sets off the steak beautifully and makes for fab sandwiches (pop on top of a slice of grilled sourdough drizzled with olive oil). Or, serve the steak French auberge style with a package of skinny French fries.

For 4 people

four 5½-ounce boneless beef top sirloin or
    porterhouse steaks, beaten ½ to ¾-inch thick
2 tablespoons Boursin
2 tablespoons salted butter, softened
extra virgin olive oil
sea salt and black pepper
watercress or arugula, to serve

AT HOME
If necessary beat the steaks to the right thickness. In a small container, beat together the Boursin and butter.

ON LOCATION
Drizzle a bit of olive oil either side of the steaks, then season. Grill for 2 minutes one side for medium–rare, or 3 minutes for medium. (If cooking on a kettle or closed grill, leave the lid off and use a spatula to press down on the steak, which will enhance the stripes.) Turn the steaks, spread with the garlic butter, then grill, again uncovered, until they feel firm but have a slight give, 2 to 3 minutes, by which time the garlic butter should be well on its way to being melted. Carefully transfer the steaks to a plate and let them rest for 5 minutes. Serve with a pile of watercress or arugula.

Kit Charcoal grill (preloaded with briquettes, firelighters, matches), spatula, plate, knife and fork (optional)

FONDUE MUSHROOM BURGERS

This luxurious veggie take on the burger option also works well as a side dish with grilled chicken, lamb, or pork.

For 4 people

8 portobello mushrooms, stems trimmed level
    with caps
5½ ounces Comté or Gruyère, thinly sliced
thickly sliced pickled chiles
extra virgin olive oil
sea salt and black pepper
approx. 3 tablespoons crème fraîche
4 pita breads, to serve

AT HOME
Trim the mushrooms and slice the cheese and pickled chiles.

ON LOCATION
Drizzle some of the olive oil over either side of the mushrooms, then season. Grill, cup-side down, for 10 minutes, then turn them, fill the cavities with slivers of cheese and a heaping teaspoon of crème fraîche, and grill for another 10 minutes.

Briefly warm the pitas either side on the grill. Halve and open out the pockets. Pop a mushroom inside each one with some sliced pickled chile.

Kit Charcoal grill (preloaded with briquettes, firelighters, matches), spatula

POOLSIDE SHRIMP

Poolside, seaside, riverside—almost any picnic that involves nearby water has the added allure of swimming thrown in. As a child there was a large open-air 1930s swimming pool close to where we lived, unheated, which meant that on the average beautiful Sunday morning we had it all to ourselves. My father used to take my brothers and me there on a regular basis for a swim followed by a breakfast picnic of pink-frosted sugar buns and tea on the lawn that sloped down to it. My adult taste might have migrated to the savory scent of shrimp shells toasting over hot coals, but the experience is one and the same. It is the shell that encapsulates that bisque-like scent that infuses the shrimp within. There is no need to think further than an envelope of salt in which to dip them as they are peeled. And if you do happen to be on a beach, if you are after the perfect chain of events, then stroll down to the water to wash your fingers, taking some really ripe mangoes or peaches, and lie in the shallows to eat them.

For 4 to 6 people

18 ounces raw unpeeled large tiger shrimp
sea salt
Marinade
1 teaspoon fennel seeds
1 tablespoon lemon juice
2 tablespoons extra virgin olive oil
1 teaspoon finely chopped medium-hot red chile

AT HOME

Grind the fennel seeds in a pestle and mortar. In an airtight container, combine the fennel with the rest of the ingredients. Add the shrimp, close, and give it a few shakes to coat them, then chill until leaving.

ON LOCATION

Just before grilling, season the shrimp with salt, close the container, and turn it a few times. Grill until pink and firm when pressed, 1 to 2 minutes each side. Eat with your fingers as an appetizer with drinks.

Kit Charcoal grill (preloaded with briquettes, firelighters, matches), tongs

HOT DOGS FROM HEAVEN

Sausage provides one of the great no-hassle solutions to entertaining any number of people, and they are international; pretty much every country has its own take on sausage. The ideal here is to grill up lots of different types: juicy prime pork, venison, or wild game, Bratwurst and Frankfurters, Toulouse, Merguez, and the like. Then dish them up with a pile of bread and a few relishes, and you have some serious hot dog heaven.

Vegetarians needn't despair. Look for some premium vegetarian sausage, or grill up some of the Fondue Mushroom Burgers (see page 139). You can fit a fair amount of sausage on a portable grill, enough for 6 to 8 people, and they cook sufficiently quickly that you should be able to fit several batches in while the coals are hot, within the space of about an hour.

Hot dog buns are an obvious vehicle, but markets in France that set you the challenge of going inside without succumbing to the lure of the foot-long meaty sausage grilling at the entrance invariably take it no further than a length of baguette, finished with a squeeze of ketchup and of mustard. And they are quite the best hot dogs around.

All the following recipes serve 6 to 8 people

2¾ pounds sausage—a selection of any you like: Toulouse, pork, venison, wild game, Merguez, Frankfurters

Without pricking the sausage, lay them on the grill rack spaced about ¾ inch apart to ensure they caramelize evenly. The exact time it will take for each type of sausage to cook will depend, about 20 to 30 minutes in total. Tend them assiduously—they can easily color and burn, so move any that are cooking quickly to the outside. Remove the sausage as they are cooked and keep warm, covered with foil if you have some.

BREADS

Pile 'em high—in a wicker tray lined with a linen napkin or dish towel, or a big bamboo plate. My favorites for hot dogs are baguettes, pita pockets, and soft torpedo-shaped rolls.

ROASTED RED ONIONS

Heat the oven to 375°F. Lay 2 pounds peeled, halved, and sliced **red onions** in a thin layer on two cookie sheets, breaking the slices into rings as far as possible. Drizzle over a bit of **extra virgin olive oil** and roast for 35 minutes, stirring halfway through to ensure they caramelize evenly. Place them in a bowl and toss with a teaspoon of **red wine vinegar** and some **sea salt** and **black pepper**. Wrap in foil to transport, rewarming the package for a few minutes on either side on the grill to freshen them.

MUSTARD SAUCE

Whisk together 1⅓ cups **sour cream**, 4 heaping teaspoons **Dijon mustard**, a few drops of **lemon juice**, and **sea salt**.

HOT DOG ESSENTIALS

Take some **Oven-baked Sweet Tomato and Chile Relish** (see page 58; this oven-baked version is speedier than most recipes) and **ketchup**. I wouldn't even think of making your own; the assembled company will only silently remonstrate that it's not the real thing, and it does at least come in plastic bottles. Some **salad greens**, such as **arugula or watercress**, pack a nice punch to counterbalance all that meatiness.

Kit Charcoal grill (preloaded with briquettes, firelighters, matches), tongs, knife, spoon (for chilli jam)

"Dish up the sausage with a pile of bread and a few relishes, and you have some serious hot dog heaven."

A HAPPY ENDING

The most relaxing picnics are a

slow but steady transition from vertical to sitting, to lying gazing up at a canopy of leaves with something sweet in hand. However rough the affair, that small but sugary ending provides a note of civilization, a reminder of a progression of courses that we might anticipate in a restaurant or as a part of dinner at home. So, this is a big chapter, not least because so many picnics take in tea as well as dessert, so we need lots of ideas for cookies and cakes as well as easy finales.

Not that you have to get baking. Plenty of treats come ready at the start, such as a chilled bar of chocolate—one of those monster ones should silence any juniors—while my own idea of no-cook heaven is a carton of locally grown strawberries or blueberries purchased on the morning from the street market. But I also can't quite resist a bit of cooking on site; well, perhaps cooking is too grand a word for the sort of mashing and stirring to a mess that I had in mind. There are all manner of yummy creations that can be whipped up from a bag of meringues, some berries, and a tub of crème fraîche, thick cream, or mascarpone—the essentials for a rustic Eton Mess. Or forgo all that and serve the ingredients separately—by way of a deconstructed dessert that can be assembled on a plate for passing around once you are there.

Beyond this, all sorts of cakes and cookies can play a part. Anything that comes in a paper liner is ideal. We can live without cupcakes and all that frosting, but little chocolate crispies are perfect, or English flapjacks—ever my default last-minute solution. The salt caramel ones (see page 158) are wolfed down in our house. Sheet cakes are also brilliant—take them in their pan and it doubles as a serving plate, and they spread to any number of people. Springform cake pans too provide a means of transporting and protecting a cake, until you get there when the collar is easily slipped off and the bottom again stands in as a plate. Loaf cakes are also pretty friendly, in which case wrap them in foil or plastic wrap and slice them to order. Plain as it is, a Madeira can be married with any seasonal fruit, and offers an excuse to slip a half bottle of sweet wine into the cooler bag.

And just occasionally, when the call is for a "proper dessert," something to tackle with a spoon, I would opt for a colorful gelatin dessert made in silicone muffin molds, or more decadently make a tiramisu in a large clip-top canning jar.

"My own idea of no-cook heaven is a carton of locally grown strawberries or blueberries purchased on the morning from the street market."

LET'S GO: FINALES

A BAR OF CHOCOLATE

If you plan on nothing else for dessert, then a bar of chocolate (or several) is a must. If it is a mega bar, then a spell in the fridge before you leave is a good idea. And if it is a thin bar or bars, then I would pop it into the freezer to preserve that crisp bite. Frozen chocolate always brings back memories of leaving a bar of Milka on the balcony on skiing holidays in Austria as a child—by far the high point of the trip.

TURKISH DELIGHT

You want the real thing here, generous jellied cubes headily scented with rose water and liberally dusted with confectioners' sugar.

BAKLAVA

Anything involving honey is risky on a picnic and likely to cause more pain than pleasure once it starts to attract unwanted winged friends, but some **baklava** stashed in a white cardboard box will see to the craving for something sticky to go with any fruit.

MACARONS

Very Marie Antoinette, and as we know what was good enough for her… The buttercream in these does render them on the fragile side, but a patisserie box full of pastel-hued **macarons** completes any lineup of summer fruits, such as **cherries**, **strawberries**, **raspberries**, **figs**, **plums**, and **peaches**.

DATES WITH GORGONZOLA

Slit fudgy **Medjool dates** and fill with a gooey **Gorgonzola dolce**.

WATERMELON WITH FETA

Hack a small **watermelon**, preferably unseeded, into crescents and dish up with a slab of **feta**. You could build on this combination with **green olives** and **prosciutto ham**, too, and offer it up as an amuse bouche.

PEARS WITH PARMESAN

Any juicy ripe **pears** will do here, **Comice or Concorde**, that go hand in glove with a crumbly aged **Parmesan** that's been hacked into nibs.

FIGS WITH GOAT CHEESE

The faint sourness of a young **goat cheese** and a touch of salt bring out the fragrance of ripe **figs**.

MANCHEGO WITH QUINCE CHEESE

A sliver of grainy **Spanish Manchego** with an even finer sliver of perfumed **membrillo** is a classic. Throw in some crisp **roasted almonds** to share in the cultural heritage.

APPLES WITH CHEDDAR

We're so spoilt for choice of fruits today that munching on an apple can seem banal. But the finer **apple** varieties eaten with a **premium or artisan cheddar** makes for rarefied grazing, and a picnic allows us the time and space to savor them. A **mature Gouda** also marries beautifully with slivers of apple; throw in some **walnuts** and you'll have a light meal. In fact, you can wheel this one out as a big splash with different varieties of apple and a couple of cheeses (**Cantal** is another good one), and in the late summer or early fall sunshine include a bottle of **Calvados** or other fiery liquor.

IN A MESS

SUN-BAKED BANANAS

I am not the first to try to harness the heat given off by engines and automobiles as a secondary source of energy. My late father-in-law Tony Bell, who was drafted into Caen just after D-Day, enjoyed fine lunches of chicken roasted on the exhaust box of his Churchill tank as they slowly made their progression to Arnhem and then the Black Forest. It's unlikely that you're picnicking in a tank, but should you have driven to the location on a hot day (say 73°F or above), point the hood into the full sun and turn that negative "too hot to pack any chocolate" into a positive.

Before leaving home, individually wrap unpeeled **bananas** in foil, and transport a bar of **semisweet, bittersweet, or milk chocolate**. On arriving at your destination, open up the package, slit the banana, and pop a row of chocolate down the center, then position the bananas with the foil open on the dashboard and let stand until the chocolate has melted, 30 to 60 minutes. A tub of **crème fraîche** in the cooler bag and dessert's done.

BANANA FOOL

Pack a tub of **crème fraîche** in the cooler bag, and take some **bananas** and a small envelope of **brown sugar**. Slice the bananas into a large bowl, add about a third of the amount of crème fraîche, and combine, then sprinkle over some sugar.

STRAWBERRY CREAMS

Gariguette strawberries and their ilk, or wild ones, are heart-stoppingly tender. They have only a day's shelf-life once ripe if you are lucky—they collapse at the touch of a fork or spoon—which makes them perfect for a heady whipped-up summer cream. Otherwise, ensure your berries are ripe to the point of melting, and let stand in the sun once you arrive to soften them more.

Pack a tub of **mascarpone** in the cooler bag and take a carton of very ripe small **strawberries**—you want equal quantities of both. In a large bowl, hull and mash half of these with the mascarpone using a spoon or fork, adding **confectioners' or vanilla sugar** to taste, then fold through the remainder, and scoop up with **dessert cookies**.

ETON MESS

Take a bag of **meringues**, a carton of **raspberries**, and a tub of **crème fraîche**. Come dessert time, layer these in a large bowl, starting with crushed meringues, then cream, and then fruit. Repeat this depending on how many mouths there are to feed.

STRAWBERRY SHORTCAKE

Take a carton of **strawberries** and let these warm in the sun on your arrival, and pack a tub of **crème fraîche** in the cooler bag, and also take some good **shortbread**. Arrange these together on a large plate for everyone to assemble their own strawberry shortcake.

PEACH MELBA ON A PLATE

Pack some ripe **peaches** and **raspberries** and let these warm in the sun on your arrival. Pop a tub of **mascarpone** in the cooler bag and arrange halved peaches with the raspberries and the mascarpone on a large plate for passing around.

TRIFLE ON A PLATE

Pack up a bag of **amaretti** and some ripe **apricots**, which have a particular affinity with these almond-scented cookies, and let the fruit warm in the sun on arrival. Also pack a tub of **mascarpone** in the cooler bag. Serve the fruits, halved and pitted, with a pile of amaretti and the tub of mascarpone to dip into on a large plate.

ALL-AMERICAN CHERRY PIE

It's the cartoon glamour of a cherry pie that is the attraction, an icon of wholesome American living, loaded with feel-good factor and comfort. Produce a homemade cherry pie and a pile of enamel plates at the end of your picnic and you can pretty much get away with buying in whatever comes before it. This pie is quite sturdy and picnic-friendly, and the way the crust settles over the cherries looks like a sugary moonscape.

For 6 people

Crust
¾ cup plus 2 tablespoons unsalted butter,
  softened
¾ cup unrefined superfine sugar, plus extra
  for dusting
2 medium eggs
3 cups plus 3 tablespoons all-purpose flour,
  sifted

½ cup ground almonds
milk, for brushing
Cherries
1¼ pounds cherries, pitted
a generous squeeze of lemon juice
⅓ cup light brown sugar
1 tablespoon all-purpose flour

Make the crust: Creaming the butter and sugar in a food processor or stand mixer will make light work of this. Add the eggs, then gradually add the flour and ground almonds and bring the dough together. Wrap it in plastic wrap, pat into a block, and chill for at least 2 hours—it will keep for several days.

Preheat the oven to 400°F. Let the dough come to room temperature, 15 to 30 minutes, then knead it until pliable. On a lightly floured work surface, thinly roll out two thirds of the dough. Use this to line the bottom and side of a 9-inch tart/quiche pan 1¼ inches deep. Don't worry if the dough tears and you end up partly pressing it into the pan. Trim the side.

Toss the cherries with the lemon juice, brown sugar, and the flour, then place them in the tart shell, spreading them out evenly. Roll out the remaining dough, incorporating any spare trimmings, paint the pastry rim in the pan with milk, and lay it over the top. Press the pastry edges together and trim the side, then crimp the edge using the tip of your finger or else the tip of a knife. Cut a couple of small slits in the center. Brush the surface of the pastry with milk and dust with superfine sugar. Bake the pie for 30 to 35 minutes, until the pastry is golden and the cherries are tender. Transport in the tart pan, loosely covered with foil.

Kit Pie server or sharp knife, plate, fork

ORCHARD SHORTCAKE PIE

This deep fluffy blackberry and apple pie is as much about the crumbly layers of shortcake as the fruit filling. You can serve this as a cake as well as a dessert.

For 8 people

Crust
1¾ cups self-rising flour, sifted
½ heaping cup unrefined superfine sugar
1 cup confectioners' sugar, sifted
1 cup unsalted butter, diced
5 medium egg yolks
1 teaspoon vanilla extract
1 egg yolk beaten with 1 teaspoon water

Filling
14 ounces apples, peeled, quartered, cored and sliced
1½ cups blackberries
2 tablespoons unrefined superfine sugar

Make the crust: Place the flour, the two sugars, and butter in the bowl of a food processor and blitz until the mixture is crumb-like. In a bowl, beat the egg yolks with the vanilla, then add to the dry ingredients and pulse to a soft, sticky dough. Wrap in plastic wrap and chill for an hour.

Preheat the oven to 375°F, and grease an 8-inch cake pan at least 2¾ inches deep with a removable bottom. Press half the dough into the pan, laying a sheet of plastic wrap over the top and smoothing it with your fingers.

In a bowl, toss the apples and blackberries with the sugar and scatter over the bottom of the pie shell.

Roll out the remainder of the dough on a well-floured work surface (it will still be quite sticky) into a circle fractionally larger than the cake pan. Lay this on top of the fruit and press it into place, tidying the edge using your fingers. Liberally paint the surface with the eggwash and bake for 1 hour, until deeply golden, crusty, and risen. Run a knife around the collar and let cool, then transport in the pan, loosely covered in foil.

Kit Pie server or sharp knife, plate

ALMOND MADEIRA

I cannot be the only person in the world who adores a simple, lightly scented cake that subtly tastes of the sum of its parts—butter, sugar, eggs, and, in this case, almonds. But the fashion for heavily frosted cupcakes has all but done away with this genre. At a picnic there is a real call for such a cake, with no risk of melting or smothering everything in contact with sticky goo. It also works as a basic for any number of "on site desserts" as well. Team it with fragrant raspberries or strawberries and a dollop of thick cream for an elegant dessert, or eat it with crisp squares of bittersweet chocolate and some juicy cherries.

Makes one 8½-inch/5½-cup loaf

¾ cup plus 1 tablespoon unsalted butter, softened and diced, plus extra for greasing
¾ cup plus 2 tablespoons unrefined superfine sugar
4 medium eggs, separated
½ teaspoon almond or vanilla extract

1¼ cups ground almonds
1 cup all-purpose flour, sifted
2 teaspoons baking powder, sifted
¼ cup slivered almonds
confectioners' sugar, for dusting

Preheat the oven to 375°F and grease a 8½-inch/5½-cup nonstick loaf pan. In a food processor, cream the butter and sugar together, then incorporate the egg yolks and the almond or vanilla extract. Work in the ground almonds, flour, and baking powder, then transfer the mixture to a large bowl. In another large bowl, whip the egg whites until stiff, then fold into the cake batter in three batches.

Transfer the batter to the cake pan, smoothing the surface. Scatter over the slivered almonds and bake for 55 to 60 minutes, until golden and firm when pressed, and shrinking from the sides. Run a knife around the edge of the cake, let cool, and then liberally dust with confectioners' sugar. It should keep well for several days in an airtight container.

Kit Sharp knife, plate, fork

FINANCIERS

It took me a long time to embrace silicone baking molds, until I realized they were the answer to turning out perfect financiers, and pretty much any shape that takes your fancy will do here. If you are making them in a nonstick mini muffin pan, then be sure to grease it well and run a knife around the edge of the cakes as soon as they come out of the oven.

The batter for these needs to be made ideally the night before, which fits in perfectly with most preparations. They are accommodating little sponges that can be studded with pieces of any fruit or berry, or chocolate chips, should you desire.

Makes approx. 24

1¹/₃ cups confectioners' sugar, sifted
²/₃ scant cup ground almonds
5½ ounces egg whites (4 to 5 medium eggs)
1 tablespoon honey
6 tablespoons unsalted butter, melted
   and cooled
½ teaspoon vanilla extract

½ cup plus 1 tablespoon all-purpose flour, sifted
½ teaspoon baking powder, sifted
raspberries, blueberries, ½-inch pieces of peeled
   apple or apricot, bittersweet chocolate chips,
   to decorate

Combine the confectioners' sugar and ground almonds in a large bowl, add the egg whites, and whisk to blend, then add the honey, butter and vanilla, then the flour and baking powder. Cover and chill for at least half a day, but ideally overnight.

Preheat the oven to 425°F. If using a mini muffin pan, then grease well with butter; there is no need if using silicone molds. Fill three quarters full, then decorate with one or two berries (placing raspberries hole down) or pieces of fruit, depending on the size of mold, or if making chocolate ones, scatter a few chips over the top. Bake for 15 to 20 minutes, until golden and firm. Run a knife around the cakes right away, then let stand for 5 to 10 minutes before removing from the pan, or popping out of the silicone molds. Transport in an airtight container or cake tin, or in a pretty bag.

TRIPLE CHOCOLATE CRISPIES

SALT CARAMEL ENGLISH FLAPJACKS

One of our best-loved easy treats, these chocolate crispies are great if there is a posse of children to please. They come with three-chocolate appeal; halfway between bittersweet and milk, with white chocolate chips thrown in. It's worth making these with a high-end chocolate too; the difference will show.

Variation on a theme of a Brit favorite—the flapjack. These naturally lend themselves to the charm of salt caramel, with salted butter and dulce de leche (or Nestlé's Carnation Caramel) in lieu of golden syrup. It takes about as long to whip these up as to make a cup of tea. In fact, I usually don't bother with the chocolate drizzle, but it makes a nice finishing touch.

Makes approx. 14

Makes 25 squares

3½ ounces milk chocolate, broken into pieces
3½ ounces bittersweet chocolate (approx. 70 percent cocoa solids), broken into pieces
2 tablespoons unsalted butter
4¼ cups Rice Krispies
2 rounded tablespoons white chocolate chips

1 cup plus 1 tablespoon lightly salted butter, diced
¾ cup plus 2 tablespoons light brown sugar
1 cup dulce de leche (or Nestlé's Carnation Caramel)
4 cups rolled oats
1¾ ounces bittersweet chocolate (approx. 50 percent cocoa solids), broken into pieces

In a large heatproof bowl set over a pan with some gently simmering water in it, melt the milk and bittersweet chocolate with the butter, then stir in the Rice Krispies. Arrange about 14 paper liners in one or two mini muffin pans and fill with heaping tablespoons of the mixture. Scatter a few chocolate chips over each and chill until set, 30 to 60 minutes, then store in an airtight container to transport.

Preheat the oven to 350°F. In a medium saucepan, gently melt the butter with the sugar and caramel over medium heat and beat until smooth and amalgamated. Stir in the oats, then transfer the mixture into a 9-inch square brownie pan or equivalent-size baking pan, pressing it down using the back of a metal spoon, and bake for 20 minutes, until very lightly colored.

Let cool for about 30 minutes. In a heatproof bowl set over a pan with some gently simmering water in it, melt the chocolate and drizzle over the flapjack. Let stand for several hours for the chocolate to set, then cut into 25 squares. Wrap in foil or stack in a cake tin to transport.

FARMHOUSE GOLDEN RAISIN CAKE

Golden raisins are the most succulent and sweet of all dried grapes, and this lightly fruited cake has hearty outdoor spirit without being overly heavy. Wheel it out at teatime on an all-day picnic, once you've exhausted the ball games or sandcastle-building on the beach and hunger is starting to bite. It's also just the ticket with a sip of port or sherry on a crisp autumnal morning before going off on a ramble. And like most fruit cakes, it finds a natural friend in a sliver of cheddar or other hard cheese.

Makes one 8-inch cake

1¹⁄₃ cups all-purpose flour
1²⁄₃ cups ground almonds
3 teaspoons baking powder
1 heaping teaspoon apple pie spice
¾ cup plus 1 tablespoon light brown sugar
²⁄₃ cup unsalted butter, diced

4 medium eggs
3 tablespoons milk
2 cups golden raisins
½ scant cup chopped candied peel
dark rum, for brushing
superfine sugar, for dusting

Preheat the oven to 325°F. In a food processor, combine the flour, ground almonds, baking powder, spice, and sugar, add the butter, and pulse to a fine crumble. Now incorporate the eggs and then the milk. Transfer the batter to a large bowl and fold in the golden raisins and candied peel.

Grease and line with parchment paper both the bottom and the side of a 8-inch round cake pan 2¾ inches deep—you can use a dab of the cake batter to glue the side ends in place. Spoon the batter into the prepared pan, mounding it in the center, and bake for about 1¼ hours, or until a toothpick inserted into the center comes out clean. Liberally brush the top of the cake with rum and dust with superfine sugar using a strainer. Let cool, then unmold and peel away the paper. Unlike many fruit cakes this is good eaten immediately. Wrap in foil or pop into a cake tin to transport.

Kit Sharp knife

DATE BROWNIES

Having featured brownies in pretty much every single book I have written involving sweet stuff, I wasn't going to include them here. But when it came to a rushed end of summer picnic, I happened to have some of these in the freezer, and they went down so well I felt they had to be squeezed in, even if it does mean there is now a ridiculous amount of chocolate in this chapter. The dates make the brownies even stickier than usual, well on their way to being a parfait once they are soft.

Makes one 9-inch pan of brownies

10½ ounces bittersweet chocolate (50 percent cocoa solids), broken up, plus 3½ ounces (70 percent cocoa solids), chopped
¾ cup plus 1 tablespoon lightly salted butter, diced
¾ cup plus 1 tablespoon light brown sugar
4 medium eggs, and 1 egg yolk
1 cup plus 2½ tablespoons ground almonds
¾ cup plus 1 tablespoon all-purpose flour
3 tablespoons unsweetened cocoa
1 rounded teaspoon baking powder
3 tablespoons strong black coffee
3½ ounces Medjool dates, halved lengthwise, pitted, and sliced across
confectioners' sugar, for dusting

Preheat the oven to 325°F. You need a 9-inch square brownie pan 1½ inches deep, or an equivalent-size baking pan. Provided it is nonstick there is no need to butter and flour it. In a heatproof bowl set over a pan with some gently simmering water in it, melt the 50 percent cocoa chocolate with the butter. Remove from the heat, add the sugar, and beat to get rid of any lumps.

Add the eggs and yolk to the chocolate mixture one by one and beating after each addition, continuing to beat at the end until the mixture is very glossy and amalgamated. Gently fold in the ground almonds, then sift over the flour, cocoa, and baking powder and fold in without overmixing. Stir in the coffee and then fold in two thirds of the 70 percent cocoa chocolate and the dates, separating out the pieces.

Pour the chocolate mixture into the pan and scatter the rest of the chopped chocolate over the top. Bake for 25 to 30 minutes, until the outside of the cake is risen and slightly cracked; a toothpick inserted into this section should come out with just a few gooey crumbs, and likewise in the center. Run a knife around the edge of the pan and let the cake cool, then chill for several hours or overnight. Lightly dust with confectioners' sugar and slice into 25 squares.

POLKA DOT COOKIES

You're never too old for chocolate M&Ms, and these blowsy crisp cookies are sure to brighten any picnic blanket.

Makes approx. 10 to 12 big cookies

½ cup plus 1 tablespoon unsalted butter, diced
⅓ cup plus 1 tablespoon unrefined
  superfine sugar
3 tablespoons golden syrup or dark corn syrup

1 teaspoon vanilla extract
1⅓ cups plus 2 tablespoons all-purpose flour
½ teaspoon baking powder
½ teaspoon baking soda
vegetable oil, for brushing
2½ packets of M&Ms

In a food processor, cream the butter and sugar together until pale and fluffy, then add the syrup and vanilla. Sift the flour, baking powder, and baking soda together, add to the butter and sugar mixture, and process to a dough. Remove the dough and wrap in plastic, then chill for at least 30 minutes.

Preheat the oven to 400°F and lightly oil two cookie sheets.

Form the dough into balls the size of a walnut and gently flatten them between your palms into chubby disks about 2 inches in diameter. Arrange these spaced well apart on the cookie sheets and bake for 12 to 14 minutes, until evenly golden and slightly risen.

While still warm, press the M&Ms into the surface, one in the center and six around the outside. Let the cookies cool for 5 minutes, then loosen them with an offset spatula and let cool completely. They keep well for several days in an airtight container. It is a good idea to transport them neatly stacked—if you shake them around, the M&Ms are likely to come loose.

SALT CARAMEL MILLIONAIRE'S SHORTBREAD

I can think of several children forced to name their all-time favorite cookie or cake who would without hesitation say "millionaire's shortbread," although not just any old millionaire's; it's got to be homemade. The offer here has the promise of a good chocolate along with a caramel with a hint of salt. The white chocolate marbling is pretty, though not essential.

Makes one 9-inch square pan

Shortbread
1 cup unsalted butter, chilled and diced
½ cup unrefined superfine sugar
1½ cups plus 2 tablespoons all-purpose flour
1 cup plus 2 tablespoons ground almonds
1 teaspoon vanilla extract

Caramel
7 tablespoons unsalted butter

⅓ cup unrefined superfine sugar
1 tablespoon golden syrup or dark corn syrup
1 cup plus 2 tablespoons dulce de leche
  (or Nestlé's Carnation Caramel)
⅓ level teaspoon fine sea salt

Top
7 ounces bittersweet chocolate (approx. 50 percent
  cocoa solids), broken into pieces
2 rounded tablespoons white chocolate chips
  (optional)

Make the shortbread: In a food processor, pulse all the shortbread ingredients to a dough. Grease a 10¾-x-7-inch baking pan or 9-inch square brownie pan and press the dough into the bottom—you can lay a sheet of plastic wrap over the top to help smooth it. Prick with a fork, loosely cover with plastic wrap, and chill for at least 1 hour.

Preheat the oven to 300°F and bake the shortbread straight from the fridge for 45 minutes, until very lightly colored. Let cool.

Make the caramel: In a small nonstick saucepan, bring all the caramel ingredients to a boil, stirring until melted and amalgamated. Simmer very gently for 8 to 9 minutes, stirring frequently, then pour over the shortbread and let cool for at least an hour until set, but overnight is even better.

In a heatproof bowl set over a pan with some gently simmering water in it, melt the bittersweet chocolate and smooth in a thin layer over the top of the caramel. If you want to marble the surface, melt the white chocolate in the same way, then drop ¼ teaspoons on top of the dark and marble by swirling with a toothpick. You have to work quite quickly here—if, for any reason, the dark chocolate starts to set, then you can pop it momentarily into a low oven until it softens again.

Set aside in a cool place until set but still soft, then cut into squares (a small serrated knife is best for this), let set completely in a cool place, and chill. This sweet offering will keep well in a covered container for several days somewhere cool.

Kit Sharp knife

MELTING MOMENTS

Piled high on a plate, these little cakes are worthy of a place at the Mad Hatter's tea party in *Alice's Adventures in Wonderland*. It's basically a type of shortbread that is true to its name, but with a bit of jam on top they have cake-like appeal. If you want something in a paper liner but don't want to rustle up cupcakes, then these fit the bill. They're also egg free, so perfect for anyone with an allergy.

Makes 14 to 17 cakes

²/₃ cup unsalted butter, diced
²/₃ cup confectioners' sugar, sifted, plus extra
   for dusting
finely grated zest of 1 lemon

3 tablespoons cornstarch, sifted
1¼ cups self-rising flour, sifted
1 to 2 tablespoons seedless raspberry jam

Preheat the oven to 375°F. In a food processor, cream the butter, sugar, and lemon zest together, then incorporate the cornstarch and flour. You should have a soft squishy dough.

Arrange about 14 to 17 paper liners inside one or two mini muffin pans. Roll the dough into balls the size of a walnut and, using your finger, indent a shallow hole into each one. Place these hole-up in the liners, gently pressing them onto the bottom to steady them. Bake for 15 to 17 minutes, until lightly colored, then remove and let cool. Note: If you're using two pans, the lower one may take a bit longer to bake than the top.

Drop a spoonful of jam into the center of each cake to fill the holes, and lightly dust with confectioners' sugar using a tea strainer. Set aside for an hour or two for the jam to set slightly. Transport to your picnic on a plate or in a cake tin. The cakes will keep well for up to a week in a sealed container.

LAVENDER SHORTBREAD

This shortbread derives from Castle Farm in Kent, England, which cultivates swathes of different kinds of lavender. Its slightly astringent perfume makes for a very particular shortbread, here using ground rice, which gives it a lovely grainy finish. As a child I remember ground rice was a regular milky pudding on the table along with rice pudding, but these days this ingredient is most likely to be found in Indian markets. Failing that, you can grind your own using a coffee grinder, in which case the finer the better.

Makes 18 fingers

$^2/_3$ cup lightly salted butter, softened
$^1/_3$ cup plus 1 tablespoon superfine sugar,
  plus extra for dusting
15 drops lavender extract for baking
1$^1/_4$ cups all-purpose flour
$^1/_2$ cup ground rice
finely grated zest of 1 lemon
a pinch of dried or fresh lavender flowers, plus
  extra for decorating (optional)

Preheat the oven to 325°F and line a 10¾-x-7-inch baking pan with parchment paper, taking it up the sides.

In a large bowl, cream the butter, sugar, and lavender extract together using a hand mixer, then add the flour, ground rice, lemon zest, and lavender flowers and beat until the dough is crumbly. Press this into the lined pan without totally compressing and leaving it quite crumbly. Bake for 30 to 35 minutes, until pale gold, then remove and dust with superfine sugar.

Let cool and then cut into fingers. You can also scatter over a few more lavender flowers.

BLACK FOREST FRIDGE CAKE

Of all the biscuits that can be used to make a fridge cake, nothing satisfies quite like a Graham cracker— or Sables Anglais L'Original as the French would have it, which gives them a much more glamorous spin. It's that wholesome grainy finish that spars with the silky chocolate surrounding it. Add in juicy candied cherries and we are deep in the Black Forest country.

Makes 25 squares

10½ ounces bittersweet chocolate (approx.
    70 percent cocoa solids), broken into pieces
¾ cup plus 1 tablespoon lightly salted butter,
    diced
1½ tablespoons golden syrup or dark corn syrup

1 cup raisins
1 scant cup candied cherries, halved
9 ounces Graham crackers, broken into
    ½ to ¾-inch pieces
confectioners' sugar, for dusting

In a large heatproof bowl set over a pan with some gently simmering water in it, melt the chocolate, butter, and syrup, stirring until smooth. Stir in the raisins, the cherries, and the crackers, tossing until everything is coated in the chocolate mixture.

Line the base of a 9-inch square brownie pan with parchment paper (you can dab a bit of the melted chocolate mixture on the four corners to make it stick), and spoon the mixture over the bottom of the pan. Lay a sheet of plastic wrap over the surface, and press it level using your hands, though it will still appear slightly craggy. Remove the plastic wrap and loosely cover with another sheet of parchment paper, then chill until hard, 2 to 3 hours.

Run a knife around the edge of the pan to remove the slab and lift off the paper. Place upward on a board and liberally dust with confectioners' sugar using a tea strainer. Cut into whatever size squares you'd like and chill. It will keep well for a good week, but you may want to give it another flurry of confectioners' sugar close to the time of serving. Transport in an airtight container or cake tin.

TIRAMISU IN A JAR

This is my default posh dessert for a picnic, ultimately transportable and chic in a clip-top Le Parfait canning jar. At your destination, simply spoon it into retro plastic or melamine cups with saucers.

For 4 people

1/3 cup plus 1 tablespoon strong black coffee, cooled
3 tablespoons Kahlua or Tia Maria
2 medium eggs, separated
1/4 cup unrefined superfine sugar
1 1/2 cups mascarpone
1 teaspoon vanilla extract
3 1/2 to 4 1/2 ounces ladyfingers
unsweetened cocoa, for dusting

In a shallow bowl, combine the coffee and liqueur. In a large bowl, whip the egg whites until they are stiff using a hand mixer. In another bowl, whip the yolks and sugar together. Beat the mascarpone into the egg yolk mixture until smooth, then the vanilla. Fold in the whipped egg whites in two batches.

Dip enough ladyfingers to cover the bottom of a 1-liter Le Parfait canning jar into the coffee-liqueur mixture until the sponge just starts to yield between your fingers, but not so that it is totally soaked, breaking them to fit as necessary. Spoon about a quarter of the mousse on top, and continue layering until you have used up all the ingredients, ending with mascarpone mousse. You should get about four layers of each. Liberally dust the surface with cocoa, close, and chill for at least 2 hours.

Kit Serving spoon, spoons

TOFFEE APPLES

Toffee apples on sticks are one of the ultimately portable sweet treats. Make a box of these to pass around as the finale to a picnic. Small apples intended for children are the ideal size; you don't want anything too hearty. A bit of cinnamon is always welcome with apples, and it is important to use a refined white superfine sugar here, otherwise the color can be hard to gauge as the caramel darkens. That aside, they are as easy as pie.

Makes 6

6 smallish apples
peanut oil, for brushing
1 1/4 cups superfine sugar
1/2 teaspoon ground cinnamon

Cut off the stems from the apples level with the fruit and insert a lollipop stick into the top of each one. Brush a cookie sheet with oil.

In a medium saucepan, gently heat the sugar until it starts to liquefy. Once about half of it has liquefied and started to color, gently stir it. Keep a careful eye on it, stirring frequently until it is a deep gold.

Remove the pan from the heat and stir in the cinnamon. Dip each apple into the caramel to coat it all over, allowing any excess to trickle back into the pan, and place bottom down on the oiled cookie sheet. The caramel should set hard within a matter of minutes. Let the apples cool completely.

CUPCAKE GELATIN DESSERTS

These refreshing little fruit juice gelatin desserts, made in colored silicone muffin molds, are great with a lunchtime spread of sandwiches and cake. Eat them with abandon—they're good for you. But you could also take a can of whipped cream.

Makes 12

5 gelatin leaves, cut into broad strips (or
   2 envelopes powdered gelatin, see below)
1¼ cups smooth fresh orange juice

a couple of squeezes of lemon juice
1¼ cups red grape juice

Divide the gelatin leaves equally among two bowls, cover with cold water, and let soak for 5 minutes, then drain. Pour 1½ tablespoons boiling water over the gelatin in each bowl and stir until it dissolves.

Spoon about 3 tablespoons of the orange juice one at a time into one of the bowls, then mix this back in with the rest of the orange juice and add a squeeze of lemon juice. In the other bowl, do the same with the grape juice.

Lay 12 silicone muffin cups out in a roasting or baking pan. Fill six with the orange gelatin solution and six with the grape gelatin solution. Chill for several hours or overnight until set. Transport in a shallow baking pan.

Powdered Gelatin
In a small bowl, sprinkle the gelatin over a few tablespoons of just-boiled water. Let stand for several minutes to soften, then stir for a minute or two, by which time you should have a clear sticky solution.

If the gelatin hasn't completely dissolved, place the bowl within another bowl of just-boiled water and let stand for a few minutes longer, then give it a good stir. Alternatively, pour the mixture into a heatproof bowl set over a pan with some gently simmering water in it, as though you were melting chocolate, and gently heat. Divide the mixture among the two bowls and follow the recipe as above.

Kit Spoons

INDEX